PUSHING UP PEOPLE

The Secret Behind One of the Most Exciting Success Stories in American Business

PUSHING UP PEOPLE

The Secret Behind One of the Most Exciting Success Stories in American Business

By Art Williams

Published by:

Parklake Publishers, Inc.
P. O. Box 4701
Doraville, Georgia 30362

Manufactured in the United States of America

Dedication

To my wife, Angela, a "dream-come-true" partner in life.

To my son Art III, and my daughter, April Ann. No daddy has ever been more proud, and no children have ever brought more joy.

A note about "the family" —
It seems that the family is under attack in the United States today. As I write this book, the divorce rate is almost 50%.

I believe that you must have your priorities straight in order to have a full, successful, and happy life. If your only goals are to be successful in business and to make a lot of money, you will grow to be a bitter old man or woman.

Don't forget your family.

Your family gives you someone to love and someone that will love you. Your family gives you someone to share your life with — all the victories and all the defeats. Through your family, you can find life's real joys and real happiness.

I wish for you a wonderful family life.

Foreword

"Pushing Up People" is the culmination of over 20 years of working with people — first as a teacher and football coach, and later as president of A.L. Williams. Both situations involved working closely with large numbers of people, learning to balance teamwork with individual success.

But that's only part of the story behind *"Pushing Up People."* Some background information on how we built our company further explains how I formed many of the "push-up principles" that I use in management and why I feel so strongly about them.

In 1977, we formed a company with seven managers and 85 people who had been marketing "buy term and invest the difference" for a national company, and who were willing to take a risk. We gave up our jobs, put the security of our families on the line and struck out to build a company based on a belief. At the time that we made our decision, we had "nothing" to get started with: no office, no compensation plan worked out, no materials to take to clients to show them the philosophy we believed in. We didn't even have a name for our company!

All we had was a group of people who felt so strongly about what they were selling and the type of company they wanted to work for, that the risk didn't matter.

Were we scared? Yes. We all knew that we might not make it. In fact, the odds were that we wouldn't. A high percentage of people who start their own business today don't make it.

That's not all we had against us. We also had people telling us that what we were doing wouldn't work. According to the "experts," we weren't building our company with the "right kind" of people. You see, we didn't try to recruit people who had already sold insurance or people who had CFPs, CLUs or fancy degrees from an important university. We recruited people like ourselves, from all walks of life. They were people who had dreamed all their lives of accomplishing something special, but didn't necessarily have the social or financial means in hand to do so.

When you add that to the fact that our philosophy was controversial, that our "buy term and invest the difference" belief was scorned by nearly every insurance company in the United States, you really start to get the picture!

But you know, A.L. Williams did make it.

In seven short years, we have grown from a company of 85 people to over 100,000. As of the end of 1984, we had produced over $61 billion worth of term life insurance. Right now we do business in 49 states and we're producing over $3 billion of insurance every month. The average size policy we sell the consumer has a face value of more than $135,000. We're helping to protect hundreds of thousands of families all across America.

And just as incredible is the individual success of the people in our company. At least 75 people in A.L. Williams are millionaires. Many more are "on target" to become millionaires. We have many managers who make, not $20,000 a year, but $20,000 a month! They operate with a sense of pride and self-esteem that comes with owning your own business.

I'm proud of what our company has done for people, but the thing that I'm the most proud of is the way we've built our company. In the end, I really believe that's the main reason for our success.

We built A.L. Williams based on the principle of treating people right, of making *all* of our decisions based on what was good for our people and our clients *first*.

When we started out with those seven managers and 85 people, we said we were going to build a company that would operate for the good of the people who worked for it.

I have always believed that you can run a company to obtain selfish goals by using intimidating management techniques only for a certain period of time. Sooner or later, the people who work for you will figure you out. They'll figure you out, and either try to cheat you back or quit. In either case, you reach a point of zero growth, or possibly bankruptcy. You wake up one day and find you've built yourself a business where maybe you're a little ashamed of the way you do things.

When we started our company, we vowed that it would never come to that. I have felt from Day One that we would manage *our* way. We would lay the whole company on the line to follow our management beliefs. We were going to treat people the way people ought to be treated. We were willing to stand by that belief...no matter what. We knew what we were doing was right. You can't replace that feeling with anything in the world. To me, no amount of money is worth the feeling I have about this company every night before I cut off the light to go to sleep.

Folks, I believe that 99 percent of all Americans would build their business that way if they knew from the start they were going to make money. But a lot of people won't even try because they don't think you can have both. They don't believe that treating other people right and helping the people who work for you to succeed is going to make you financially independent.

Well, I'm here to tell you right now that the beautiful thing about A.L. Williams is that you can have both.

In fact, we have built our company in such a manner so that the *only* way you can succeed is by *"Pushing Up People."*

I know it's hard to believe. A lot of people who join A.L. Williams don't see it at first. They don't really realize that they succeed by building other successful people.

I've written *"Pushing Up People"* just for that reason. I promise you that if you follow the principles and take hold of the beliefs set out in this book, that you will learn what it takes to become the kind of business man or woman you always dreamed of being — someone who is successful, but not at the expense of other people. You'll begin to establish financial independence for your family and at the same time, earn love and respect from your people.

"Pushing Up People" is for those who want to win in a career with A.L. Williams. Read it knowing that this is management philosophy that has made thousands of people successful and that this philosophy has made A.L. Williams one of the most exciting success stories in American business.

Go! Go! Go!

Art Williams

Table of Contents

Introduction

The greatest power in any business is people power. No matter how much potential your business has, no matter how good your product or service might be, the thing that will determine the success or failure of your business is the effort and the dedication of the people who make up your business "team."

Often, when new managers start out, they worry most about the technical aspects of their business. They wonder, "Do I have enough business knowledge?" "Can I make money?" Sometimes they overlook the fact that the greatest challenge of the leadership role is learning to channel the tremendous power of people.

In every business the most serious problems are people problems. Every manager knows how hard it is to keep people motivated and productive in their jobs. If your people are unhappy, unmotivated, or have attitude problems, your success and the success of your business is bound to suffer.

Somewhere along the way, American business developed the idea that the job of a manager is to make people work. That can be a problem, because people don't like to be *made* to do anything. Of course, there must be some supervision of less experienced people by those more experienced. But, in some businesses, people are valued less than the office furniture.

I believe that the thing we've lost in modern management is the human touch. Traditional schools and management place so much emphasis on profit margin and net worth that managers sometimes forget employees are human beings with their own set of hopes, desires, and needs. They forget that they were once "just an employee" themselves.

Too often, managers think that the success and profitability of their business comes first, and the success of their people second. I believe that it works just the opposite. You show people how they can succeed, help them to achieve personal success, and your own success and the success of your company is assured.

Your people are your company's most important asset. It is their contribution that makes the difference between your company's success or failure.

My years as a football coach taught me about teamwork. I learned that no one person on any football team is more important than any other person. The quarterback may call the plays, he may be the official team leader, but he cannot do his job without the commitment and cooperation of each of his 10 teammates. A football team's chance of victory is only as good as its weakest player. If any one of these people does badly, the success of the entire team is jeopardized.

The same is true in business. In our sales company, for example, the newest recruits are just as important to the long range success of the company as the experienced managers and administrators. The new reps are the experienced managers of the future, and if they do not succeed today, there will be trouble in years to come. The failure of every new member of the company becomes a potential loss of leadership down the road.

That belief that the new members of our company are tomorrow's leadership team is why I never call people in our company "employees." We don't have managers and employees. We have leaders and potential leaders.

In a recent interview on CBS' "60 Minutes," Admiral Grace Jones of the U.S. Navy made a wise statement about the difference between "management" and "leadership." "Managers manage things, leaders lead people," she said.

I agree totally. The art of "people management" requires that the manager assume the responsibilities of leadership. Leaders have a responsibility to help people achieve personal goals, in addition to the goals of the company or department. They have a responsibility to lead their people in a way that helps to build their strengths and compensate for their weaknesses. And, above all, they have a responsibility to help their people succeed.

Young managers starting out need to understand the power of leadership. They need to realize that their influence is significant. Strong leaders mean everything to a company's success and the success of individual people. As a leader, you can make *all* the difference in the careers of the people who work with you. Your leadership can result in your people achieving personal success and even financial independence. Or, if you don't take it seriously, it can result in personal failure for your people and business failure for you.

Being a leader doesn't come naturally to most people. Concern for others and the ability to put the needs of your people before your own sometimes have to be learned.

The purpose of this book is to talk about leadership, and to introduce you to the basic principles of a kind of "management" that I believe will succeed for you and your people better than any other. I know it works. I have personally witnessed its results in my business life time and time again. I know that it can help you and your company or department.

For many of you, it will be a new way of thinking that may take some getting used to. If you've been managing the traditional way, it may even go against your grain for awhile. But I encourage you to lead on.

In this book, I've listed some common "management mistakes." You may see yourself in these areas. But I've also included some leadership principles that I believe should take the place of those mistakes. I've called them "Push-Up Principles" to remind you of your ultimate goal of helping to push up others. I promise you that if you practice these "push-ups" every day on the job (and off the job, too), you'll see a difference in your business. There will be an excitement and an electricity in the air that you won't find in a company where everybody is fighting to hold onto their little spot. The pride you'll experience from seeing your people excel, and the personal relationships you'll build along the way, will reward you personally in a way you never dreamed.

Your people will become your family...with all the headaches and heartaches that come with family life, sure, but with all the same joys and richness of experience that come with family life, too. You'll notice the change because work will become a central pleasure in your life, not something you dread to go to each day.

Make these "push-ups" as much a part of your daily management routine as you do the push-ups you practice to keep yourself in shape.

But don't just take my word for it. Try them...watch the incredible results.

PUSHING UP PEOPLE

The Secret Behind One of the
Most Exciting Success Stories
in American Business

PART I

Basic Principles To Master In Pushing Up People

On February 10, 1977, a new kind of company was formed with the motto, "A Company Where Salespeople are King." We believed that our people were our greatest asset. We decided that we would never limit a person's opportunity, cut his territory or income or deny an earned promotion.

We had become discouraged with corporate America. We believed that it was possible to build a company by "doing what's right" for the consumer and for our own people.

From that environment, A.L. Williams was born. The original 85 pioneers began with a dream, the dream that a person of average ability on the "outside," but with the heart of a champion, could become somebody special.

The results were phenomenal. The odds against our company even surviving were tremendous. We won "big" because we believed in people and adopted a way of life that consisted of *Pushing Up People*.

Chapter 1

Everybody Wants To Be Somebody

Management Mistake

Too many managers fail to recognize their people's full potential.

Leadership Solution

Leaders recognize the hidden qualities that bring about success, and focus on the "specialness" of their people.

Everybody wants to win. You do...I do...your neighbor does. Most of the people you know are struggling to get ahead in their jobs, trying to improve their circumstances. You probably know exactly how that is.

Yet, if you're like most people, you have difficulty seeing yourself as "somebody special." Oh, you're special to your family and friends, but when you think about "being somebody," chances are you don't think about that "somebody" as you. You've read stories about great leaders in business. You've known people who seemed to have it all — the right schools, the right "connections," the right job, the right social circle — the kind of people who were *meant* to be successful. But you don't really see yourself as one of those people.

If that's true, and I believe it is for most of us, you probably don't see the people who work with you in that way, either. Chances are you've acquired the same prejudices and opinions that many people have. To be a successful manager, the first thing you must do is change that perception.

Push-Up Principle
There's more to a person than what's on his resume.

I believe that American business has come to rely too much on a set of artificial standards for judging people in the workplace. People's worth is measured by things like college board scores, I.Q. level, and the type of college degree they have (heaven help you if you don't have one!). If you want a job in management, you'd better have all the right management "credentials," or you'll be back on the street in no time.

For many years, I was devastated by this kind of thinking. I knew in my heart that I was somebody, that I had potential, and I knew I was willing to work like a maniac to get ahead. But I had my sights set pretty low. For a long time, I just couldn't see how someone with a teaching and coaching background could be a success in business.

There's a story with a message that I often tell when I speak around the country. Because I'm now the president of a very successful company, I use myself and my background as an example.

Picture this: A guy goes downtown to the biggest company in the city — one of those tall buildings with the fancy symbol on top. He goes to the personnel office and says, "I want to fill out an application." The personnel clerk looks him over suspiciously and says, "What job are you applying for, sir?" He thinks a minute and replies, "Well, let's see, what's the best job you've got around here? President? OK, I want to apply for that job."

He fills out an application and leaves. The next day, the Search Committee reviews the applications. They get to his application and they say, "Who is this guy? A teacher? A football coach? Who does he think he is, applying for president of this company? Why, he doesn't even have an MBA! Throw that in the trash can! Next application, please!"

The situation isn't as far-fetched as you might think. It's the perfect example of the strict ideas most companies in America have about who is good management material.

I know, because it happened to me. About the time I was thinking about leaving education, I drove to Atlanta, Georgia and interviewed with a job placement firm for executives. They didn't just tell me that I wasn't qualified or didn't have the potential — I never heard from them again!

Push-Up Principle

"Inside qualities" are more important than "outside qualities."

So often, people like me are made to feel like we're just not capable. We learn that all we can do is make a living, just be an "employee." We don't have the right qualities to make it to the top.

I don't believe that "outside" qualities like family background and education are the only qualities necessary to win. American history is filled with people who accomplished tremendous things without those advantages. Inside qualities count just as much — determination, character, morals, and common sense. These qualities have a power all their own, and are often more responsible for great achievements than any outer qualities.

I believe that the universities and the big businesses try to make us think that credentials are everything. Now, there's nothing wrong with higher education; I have a master's degree, and it has been valuable to me in my life, especially in terms of self-confidence. But too many times, we're led to believe that you can't succeed without those kinds of "symbols." In my business career, I've found that, sometimes, the very credentials that many people value so much can actually *inhibit* success.

Contrary to what many people think, victory doesn't always go to the smartest people. Sometimes, people who have brilliant minds can talk a good game and totally intimidate people with their intelligence. But I've found that, often, people who are exceptionally smart spend too much valuable time trying to analyze things. They read as much as they can; they look for an easier way or a quicker way or a better way. But, too often, they just don't get around to actually doing anything. I'll take a "do-er" with plain old common sense any day.

Then there are what I jokingly call "pretty people." I don't mean physically pretty, but "privileged" people, those who have had a very easy life. They grow up with an attitude that they're just a little bit better than the average folks out there, even though they may have accomplished very little on their own. Maybe they grew up with a lot of money or have a degree from a prestigious school. They develop a feeling of superiority, a feeling that life owes them. They just aren't willing to get out there and really "dig around" with the rest of us. They aren't willing to do what's necessary to win in business.

Sure, many privileged people and brilliant people do succeed in a big way. Those qualities can certainly be advantages in many situations. My point here is that many people accept those qualities as the only "right" qualities. Yet, you don't have to accept the lack of those qualities as a guarantee of failure. You can succeed just fine without them.

Push-Up Principle
Victory in the free enterprise system goes to a different kind of person than most people think.

The people I see in business who are really successful aren't geniuses; they don't sit around and think all that much; they're not necessarily the best educated or the most experienced. They are the people who want to win so badly that they just go out there and do it. Even though everybody they know has told them that they can't succeed, they just go out there and succeed anyway. They know, instinctively, that determination and perseverance are far more important than fancy methods and lofty theories.

They don't expect something for nothing, and they don't expect anything to come easy. Their method of success is simply *action*. You see, a lot of people have "millionaire" ideas, but nothing in the world is cheaper than a good idea without any action behind it. The problem is finding someone who is willing to implement it. In my experience I've learned that 99 percent of the people quit before they can do what it takes to turn their good ideas into realities.

I don't know why I'm like I am, but something inside of me won't ever let me be satisfied. It keeps saying, "Go for it! You aren't supposed to be average and ordinary, Art. You're supposed to make a difference with your life." I believe that feeling, more than anything else, was responsible for my own success.

I've learned one thing in business that I know is true: there has never been a test, and never will be a test, that can measure the heart of a man or a woman. You just can't look inside people and tell what they're capable of. The only way you can tell is to put them out on the playing field, give them a chance to prove what they can do, and offer the leadership that they need to do their best.

Push-Up Principle
The key to victory is a will to win.

I believe the one quality that's more important than all the others is a "will to win." You can't defeat a will to win. Show me a man or woman who's totally obsessed with being somebody, and I'll show you a person who can figure out a way to win. It doesn't matter how high the odds are stacked against him, and it doesn't matter how long or how hard he has to work to get there. Show me a person who wants to be somebody *bad*, so bad he can't sleep at night, and I'll show you a person who's going to go out there and build a successful career.

Now in many organizations, a "will to win" doesn't count, because it's not something you can measure with a test. But if you're going to be an effective leader, you need to learn to recognize it.

Experience has shown me that the "perfect" person to hire at any level is the person who wants to be a winner. He's not looking for a handout. All he wants is an opportunity. He can still dream, and still hope, and still make a commitment.

Many people have been so butchered up in their lives by companies and individuals that they've become cynical about everything. They think that everybody's going to do it to them, and they keep looking around the corner all the time. They can't believe that anybody will be honest with them or give them a real chance. Those kinds of people have a lot of difficulty winning.

But show me someone who is willing to go out there and take a chance one more time, willing to dream one more time, and willing to pay the price, and I'll show you a person who can do something great in the free enterprise system.

A man who started out with me in the early days of our company is one of the people who proved this philosophy to me. When we met, he was a basketball coach making $6,000 a year He had never sold anything when he joined our company as a sales rep. He was very nervous and didn't have a lot of confidence.

The first time I asked him to speak at a company gathering, he was so shaken he got sick. The second time, he almost passed out on stage.

But he wanted to be somebody, and he believed in the principles of our company, so he stuck it out. Every day, he would go out and try to make sales. I knew he was dying inside every time he went out on a sales call. He agonized over every appointment, and couldn't disguise a sense of relief when someone cancelled.

But he got up every day and went out anyway. His first year he made $5,000. Ninety-nine percent of the people would have quit then. The second year he made $9,000. He went to those appointments, and he made those presentations because he believed what he was doing was right. He got doors slammed in his face over and over again. The third year, he made $18,000. He was getting better at his business. Finally, everything clicked. The fourth year, he made $100,000, and the fifth he made a quarter of a million dollars.

Given what this man went through, most people would have quit the first week. Selling never came less naturally to anyone than it did to him. But he made a decision to give it his best shot, and he just wouldn't be denied. He had a will to win like nobody I've ever seen. Today, he's a motivational speaker, a multi-millionaire, and a sales leader whom everyone turns to for advice and guidance.

Push-Up Principle
People want more from a job than money.

I really believe that people want three things: 1) to be their own boss, 2) to control their own destiny, and 3) to work at something they believe in. I know very few people who don't have these three basic desires. They may still be "just an employee," but deep down, that's their fantasy. Every "red-blooded" American wants to stand on his own two feet; he wants to work for himself and build security for himself and his family. Those are the desires and dreams that built this country.

Many people have been so beaten down that they have forgotten those basic dreams. They went out into the work world and got shot down a few times. All those people in their childhood who told them they could be anything they wanted to be seemed to have been replaced by people who were only interested in a strict set of credentials and experience. If they didn't match up with the ideal, they were passed over.

But for most people, those dreams are still there, just waiting for someone to give them a chance to happen, just waiting to grow with a leader who understands that there's more to a person than what's on the surface.

As a leader, it's important to remember that, no matter how much their confidence might have fallen from the hard knocks they've taken, no matter how much they look to you like they'll never make it, everybody wants to be somebody. It's up to you to help bring out the talent and ability that's inside. You can make the difference in whether they win or lose, in whether or not they feel good about themselves and are proud of who they are and what they've accomplished.

Ultimately, a leader is judged by the success of the people he led during his career. If you want to become somebody special yourself, help your people to become somebody special. The more successful they become, the higher they will push you up.

Chapter 2

Treat People "Good"

Management Mistake

Most managers lead by fear and intimidation, they think that being tough is being a leader.

Leadership Solution

Leaders add the human factor to all aspects of their business.

In most areas of life, it's pretty obvious that you should "treat people good." But in the business world, it's often a different case. Too many managers think that "management" means treating people in a way they would never want to be treated themselves.

Most managers are good people by nature. And there are reasons why they behave the way they do toward their people. A lot of it has to do with tradition. People tend to pattern themselves after the managers that they've had. This is especially true of new managers.

The problem is that many people don't have very good models to follow. Too often, managers in the traditional business world have been taught to lead by threats and intimidation. It goes back to that view of the *boss* as the one who bosses others around!

Any kind of genuine caring is considered a sign of weakness. If you're "too nice," traditional managers say, your people will take advantage of you. You've got to be tough in order to win people's respect.

I don't think that's true. I firmly believe that you can be a caring, concerned person and still be firm and make tough decisions. People will respect you if you are a strong and committed leader, who lets them know that you see them as human beings, not just nameless faces.

Push-Up Principle
Fear isn't the most effective management tool.

If you want to get someone's attention, threats and intimidation will certainly do that. But if you want to build a lasting work relationship, based on mutual trust and respect, you'll do irreparable damage. You'll get results, but they'll be temporary and short-range.

In our company, for example, let's assume a salesman is not making any sales. I can call him in and "dress him down." I can say, "Look, if you don't double your sales in the next month, I'll fire you." Because I'm in charge, and because he may need the job, he might go out and work extra hard to double his sales.

But I've totally destroyed my relationship with that guy because he never knows when I'm going to pull something like that again. He doesn't have any security. And I've built a barrier of fear and resentment between us that I may never be able to cross again.

But if I took that same guy and spent that time talking about the fantastic opportunities available to him and explaining what a bright future he has if he can just get his sales up, he'll wind up going out and making three times as many sales as he would have with fear as a motivator. Plus, I've built a positive relationship in which he can continue to grow and develop.

Push-Up Principle
Management by intimidation is easy management; a leader won't take the easy way.

A good friend and senior vice president in our company worked as a computer consultant before he joined the insurance business. When a company had trouble with its complex computer system, he and his staff would go in and work out the problems. He had thirty people working with him — a big management job, to say the least. As he looks back now, he is embarrassed about some of the things he did. At the time, though, it was the only way he knew.

"I had a very traditional view of management," he told me. "I had all these people on my staff, and as far as I was concerned, they were all expendable. When one of them did something I didn't like, or had a problem on the job, I just fired him. There was always somebody else to hire, and I didn't feel that it was my responsibility to put up with any problems. I thought that meant that I was a tough manager. I hardly knew my people, much less cared about their problems or how I could help them."

So many managers today still think this way. They like the idea of what I call "macho management." They humiliate people when they make a mistake, or else they fire them on the spot.

I know you've gone into offices where you could just feel the tension in the air. You may have experienced being an employee who had to "jump to attention" when the boss entered the room. It's a terrible atmosphere, and I'm convinced that it produces tense, fearful people with lower-than-average work performance.

If you manage through fear, your people will get nervous around you after a while. They won't approach you with a problem, so the problem will just get worse. They'll be afraid to be creative or express a new idea. They won't feel like they can take a chance, because they won't want to risk your disapproval. When this happens, the people suffer, and the success of the business suffers, too.

I think management by intimidation is easy management. It's "chicken management." It's so easy to just fire somebody with a problem. It's easy to reprimand people. But you can't get the maximum out of people that way.

Push-Up Principle
Treat your people with respect.

Your people aren't numbers on your own success chart. They're real people, and they deserve to be treated that way. Most people are good people. They don't ask for a lot — just to be treated with basic courtesy and respect. Lots of people in America are fed up with being treated like kids. I've seen proof of that in our business.

For years, insurance salesmen were taught to use high-pressure, fast-talking, hard-closing sales pitches. They worked under the assumption that consumers couldn't understand the complicated business of life insurance, so they didn't even try to explain it. They just tried to overwhelm the client with a lot of facts and figures. As a result, a poll a few years ago showed insurance salesmen at the bottom of a list of respected occupations.

I didn't want our company built that way. We instituted a sales process that prevented the sales people from selling on their first visit. They used that time for explaining the product to the client. The results were incredible. People responded like you wouldn't believe to simply being treated as intelligent adults who could understand basic concepts.

Remember, your people want to be treated just like you do. They have ideas and opinions, too. Let them know that you see them as mature, intelligent adults, not as school children who need to be watched and led by an office "parent."

Push-Up Principle

There's no place for prejudice in a successful business.

A part of treating people with respect is treating people fairly in terms of opportunity. All people won't perform the same way, but a leader should offer an equal opportunity to succeed to every person in the group.

In our company, people's success is based entirely on performance, regardless of their sex and race or background. For example, we have many women leaders who have built incredible careers and incomes through high production and outstanding leadership qualities. They are judged, just like everyone else in the company, by a standard of excellence, instead of standards like male and female, black and white and so forth. In any company, that should be the *only* standard for promotions and recognition.

Occasionally, I've been approached by people in our company to schedule special meetings based on sex or ethnic background. For example, I've had requests for regional vice president meetings for women or for regional vice presidents of "minority" groups. I've always rejected these suggestions, because I believe they create an atmosphere of separateness. In our company, regional vice presidents are simply regional vice presidents, whether they're male, female, minority or majority members. The same qualifications exist for that position, regardless of sex or race, and I believe that no purpose is served by categorizing people within that group.

Don't forget that your main concern as a leader is in building a quality business with the best people you can find — regardless of their special individual characteristics — and that's *all* that's important.

Push-Up Principle
Consider the impact of business decisions on your people.

Every time you make a decision, it's obvious that you have to look at its impact on your business. Too many times, that's been the only consideration. Sure, the bottom line is important, but don't forget the "people quotient" in your decision-making process. In addition to thinking about how your decisions affect your income and profitability, you must think about how they affect your people.

For example, our company is a sales company, and sales reps work on a commission basis. The new people just getting started may be having a difficult time financially. Now, it might be simpler for us, from an administrative standpoint, to pay the sales reps once a month. There would be a lot less paperwork and we'd save on processing time.

But it would be a dumb decision from a people standpoint, because the new guys who are trying to get used to a new business and a new type of income need the reassurance of a weekly check. It's a way of measuring their progress week by week, and it helps them to see, immediately, the results of their efforts in the field. It wouldn't make much difference how we did it to the company as a whole, but you can bet it would make a difference to the rep, and the rep's satisfaction must count more with the company than saving a few dollars.

Push-Up Principle:
Commitment is a two-way street.

Traditionally, we've been taught to think that the employee is the one who must be committed to his work. Companies are famous for demanding commitment from their people, then turning against them at the first sign of a problem or a mistake.

I see so many people in management today who are always cutting down their people. They'll go have a drink with a buddy and talk about how sorry their people are, how lazy they are, how dumb they are.

You've got to be proud of your people. You can't just say the words. You've got to be sincerely excited and enthused about their success, and appreciate the efforts they make.

At all companies, people come and go. You know that not everyone you hire will last, for a variety of reasons. But when you hire a person, you've got to assume that person will be with you *for life,* and you've got to treat him or her that way. It's up to you to make the commitment to invest the time and energy to train that person, help him succeed, support his efforts, and be proud of his accomplishments.

Treat people good — and they'll return the favor through a dedication to their work and a commitment to you that you never dreamed possible.

Chapter 3

Build Personal Relationships

Management Mistake

Most managers believe that personal and business relationships don't mix.

Leadership Solution

Leaders know that strong personal relationships strengthen their business relationships.

I don't know where the traditional business community got the idea that it's a crime to have personal relationships with the people you work with every day. What could be more natural than being involved in the lives of your closest work associates?

Maybe it goes back to the idea of management by intimidation. If you're going to manage through fear, then it wouldn't do to make friends with your people. It's hard to be intimidating to someone you're close to in a personal way.

Or maybe it's that, in many businesses, the manager doesn't realize that his people are the most important ingredient in his own success. If you don't realize that important fact, it's easy to take advantage of your people and see them as unrelated to your own success.

Push-Up Principle
To build personal relationships, show your people that you care.

If you want to build any kind of serious, lasting relationship with your people, you must become a master at communicating with them about all aspects of your business and their place in it. The only way you can let them know how much you value their contribution is to show them — and tell them.

One of our company's leaders was having great difficulty communicating with his people. He's a very talented guy with tremendous business ability, but he was being held back in his career by his weak people skills. I couldn't understand it at first, because he was devoted to his people, and wanted to see them successful more than anything else. But he was just too reserved with them; he made them feel uncomfortable because he seemed too "stuck-up" to care. Over the years, it took a toll on his business.

Finally, I talked to him about it. He explained that his parents were divorced when he was very young. He took it very badly, and grew up believing that you couldn't trust anyone, that everyone was out to hurt you in some way if you got too close to them. He was a little afraid to care about people, because he had cared about people in the past who had disappointed him. He was able to care about and believe in his people up to a point, but he drew back from becoming personally involved with them. Only by working at it every day has he been able to overcome this serious problem.

Your people may mean more to you than anything else —but if you can't communicate those feelings to them, then the feelings might as well not exist, because your people will never know.

Learn to communicate your unconditional love and concern. You can't expect people to build a relationship with you without your help. You are half of the relationship, and you've got to do your part to make it meaningful. Most important, you've got to learn to communicate person-to-person on a daily basis.

Push-Up Principle
Live with people through the good times and bad times.

Anyone who's been on this earth very long knows that sometimes the closest relationships with people are built during the bad times. When people are joined in a tough situation, it often builds a closeness and understanding that doesn't happen in the good times.

The same is true with your people. You form personal relationships with your people by sticking with them when things are going bad, as well as when everything's sunny. Life is a business of momentum. Sometimes you're up, sometimes you're down. In their down times, your people need your love and support more than at any other time. Unfortunately, many managers ignore people when there's trouble; they run from their people rather than deal with their problems.

When my kids were old enough, my wife Angela and I tried to communicate our commitment to them. We said, "We want you kids to know that, in your lifetime, you're going to do something that you're not proud of, and you're going to make mistakes. But you can't make a mistake that I haven't made. And I want you to know that, sometime in your life, when you've messed up and you're counting on other people to help, many people will let you down. They won't be there and believe in you when you need them. But there's no situation you can ever be in that you can't count on your mom and dad. We might hurt, we might cry, we might be disappointed, but here are two people who are going to stand by you and fight with you to overcome your problems."

I think you've got to have that same feeling about your people at work, or something pretty close to it. You build good people in business like you build good kids — and standing by them during the tough times is one of the most important elements.

Any of you with kids at home know what I mean. They go through different stages. Sometimes they're dependent and sometimes they need their freedom. Often, they do things that test your principles and traditions.

But you can't ever put yourself in a position where you cut your children off when they disappoint you. If you give up on them when everything else is going against them, they can never trust you again. You'll break your relationship with them forever.

The same is true of your relationships with people on the job. If you stand by them and love them through their difficulties, they'll come out of the situation eventually, and you will have built a bond with them that's unbelievable.

You've got to be proud of your people when they win — and tell them so — and care about them just as much, maybe more, when they lose. Just as your kids will lose faith in you if you abandon them when they're in trouble, your people will lose faith if you desert them during hard times. And when you've lost the faith and trust of your people, you are *absolutely worthless* as a leader.

Push-Up Principle
Building personal relationships
requires "unconditional commitment."

One of our national sales directors in Texas, a very wise man, often compares the commitment you have to your people at work with the commitment you have in a marriage relationship. He calls it "unconditional commitment."

"When you marry someone," he told me, "you commit to stay with them for better or worse, through good times and bad. Sometimes you get annoyed with your spouse and sometimes you're so mad you can hardly stand it. That's human nature. There are just going to be some problems when two people are together day in and day out.

"It would be easy to just give up the first time something doesn't go your way, and a lot of people do. But unconditional commitment means you're there through the good and the bad.

"It's got to be the same way at work."

Now, you may be about to slam this book shut and say, "There's *no way* I can be committed to people who work for me like I am to my wife and kids! And I sure can't *love* my people at work that way. That's too much to ask!"

Maybe it's not easy for you. Maybe you're not the kind of person who goes around expressing his emotions all the time. I don't mean you have to go around saying, "I love you" to your people (although I don't see anything wrong with that). All I mean is that you need to develop that same caring attitude.

Just as everyone wants to see their children succeed, good managers have a personal interest in the success or failure of their people.

Push-Up Principle
Leaders really know their people, their families, their goals, their abilities, and their dreams.

The most important part of building personal relationships is really getting to know your people. I can't imagine working with someone every day and not knowing his family, his wife's name, how many children they have, and so on. A person's family is a central part of his life, and few things mean more to him than knowing that the importance of his family is recognized. The ups and downs of family life have a strong impact on business performance. If you know the families of your people, you'll know when problems occur at home and you'll be better able, as a leader, to deal with the effect of those problems on the job.

Knowing people will help you in your efforts to "push them up" as well. The closer your relationship, the better you know that person's strengths and weaknesses. Sometimes, when one of your people is having difficulty in some area, you'll be able to recognize the source of his problem, based on your knowledge of him as a person. Your job of training him and helping to build up his strengths becomes easier, and you're able to offer more help than you would if you barely knew him.

Push-Up Principle
Leaders always put their people before themselves.

I've found, from my experience, that the thing people dislike most about their jobs is working for someone else. Almost everybody has the dream of working for himself. That's one of the dreams that has made the free enterprise system the most successful in the world.

No matter what business you're in, your people see themselves as working to improve their own future —not yours. If you want to have a successful business, your people must feel that you're working for them — not that they are working for you. And it should really be that way. As a leader, your most important job is helping your people to become the best they can be and reach the absolute peak of their potential. If you're able to do that, your business will take care of itself. No one can fail with a group of independent, motivated, excited and happy people, working hard to reach their own individual goals.

Part of putting your people first is standing up for them when the situation calls for it. When I was coaching, I was pretty demanding in terms of doing things right and setting high standards. My kids would probably say I was a pretty tough coach. But one thing I never allowed was criticism of our team by anybody outside the team. Whenever we were criticized by students or townspeople or the press, I did whatever I could to oppose it. We might squabble or disagree among ourselves, but when anything negative came from outsiders, we stuck together like you wouldn't believe. We were ready to go to war for each other. I believed in complete loyalty among the team members, and that built a feeling of security in the group that held us together and built a real bond among us.

That kind of feeling is invaluable in any group of people who work together, whether on a football team or in the office. But it's only possible if your people are totally convinced that you are 100 percent for them, all the time, and will take a stand to prove it. If they think you won't defend them when the situation calls for it, they won't believe in you or follow you.

Push-Up Principle

Being right isn't good enough; your people must feel and believe that you're right.

There's a man in our company who learned this lesson the hard way. He is an honest, down-to-earth guy. One day, one of his people questioned him about what he thought was an error in the way some earnings had been calculated. The difference was only a few dollars, but the leader was very upset and lost his temper when he was questioned about it.

As it turned out, the leader's figures were correct. But it really didn't matter. His bad handling of the situation gave the impression that he was trying to pull something over on his people, and their confidence in him fell to rock bottom. You see, he hadn't done anything wrong, but he gave the impression that he had when he over-reacted to the situation. It would have been better to give up the two or three dollars in question than to lose the respect of his people.

You must always be concerned that what you do is right for your people, but you must also be concerned about how your actions appear to your people.

Your people need the strength and encouragement of a leader, but they can also use the concern and consideration of a friend. It is possible to be both. If you work on building personal relationships, your own enjoyment of work will increase when the group of people you work with are also people you know and like.

Chapter 4

The Secret — Praise And Recognition

Management Mistake

Most managers emphasize the things people do wrong.

Leadership Solution

A leader accepts people's weaknesses and rewards their strengths.

Praise and recognition are the most powerful forms of motivation. Nothing encourages people to work harder and produce quality results like having their accomplishments noticed and praised.

I call praise and recognition "the secret" because, until recently, this kind of motivation was one of the best-kept secrets in business. It's often ignored in standard management practice, but successful leaders have always known its value.

In the last few years, management has recognized the principle that great leaders — and great parents — have known all along: people respond better to praise than to punishment.

When it comes to motivation, adults are no different than kids. If you criticize your children every time they make a mistake — tell them they're no good, they're sorry, they're lazy — then you'll build kids who are unhappy, frustrated, and who feel bad about themselves.

Every child wants love and praise. If you praise kids and make them feel special, they'll be happy, self-confident and ready to conquer the world. This principle works exactly the same way with adults. And you don't have to take my word for it. Educators and psychologists have done extensive studies of what motivates people. Their results have shown that, in addition to their basic "survival" needs (a job, enough money to pay the bills, financial stability, and so forth), people also have certain "inner" needs.

Those needs are things like: 1) the need to feel that they belong to a group, 2) the need to feel appreciated, and 3) the need to feel that they are recognized for their effort.

We all have those needs at all ages. We all want to feel good about ourselves and the work we do. As a manager, it's a serious mistake to ignore those basic needs; a good leader will always be looking for a way to help his people fulfill their "inner" needs as well as their basic survival needs.

Push-Up Principle

Positive motivation is the key to pushing up people.

People work for a lot of reasons — to be their own boss, to make money for their families — but one of the main things they want from their job is recognition. I believe that part of treating people good is making them feel good about their work. The best way of doing that is by rewarding the positive things they do instead of dwelling on the errors they make.

If you want someone to succeed, you start by praising him when he begins to do things right. In our business, for example, if you want to encourage new sales reps to make sales appointments, you start talking about making appointments. When one of the new reps makes a passable number of appointments, you treat him like a hero. You take him out to lunch, tell everyone in the group about it, just generally put him on a pedestal. You may have made hundreds of appointments yourself, but you've got to remember that, to the new guy, that one contact may be the hardest thing he's ever done. He deserves to be rewarded for his achievement.

Everybody wants praise for a job well done. If you start praising for successful behavior, the person will want to get the same kind of recognition again. He'll be anxious to repeat the actions that gave him such good feelings of recognition and accomplishment. Then — and this is the important part — you won't have to *make* him go out and make more appointments. He'll be eager to do it again.

The best part about praising one person in your group is that it motivates the others. People notice praise, even when it goes to someone else, and they're quick to copy the methods of others if they think it will bring them the kind of recognition they crave.

My first year as a football coach, I took my team to a football camp in South Carolina. There were six teams at the camp, including ours. Every morning, our team got up at 6 o'clock and went on a three-mile run. We were coming back to the dorms from our workout just as everyone else was getting up and going to breakfast.

My kids got a lot of teasing from the other kids, who joked about their "crazy coach" and made fun of their morning runs.

The teams paired up twice a day for games, and we won every game we played. By Wednesday afternoon, we'd beaten all the other teams at the camp. On Thursday morning when we went out, two of the other teams were out there running, too. On Friday, all six teams were there.

That's what often happens when people see success and the recognition that goes along with it. When our team became the talk of the camp, all the other teams wanted to copy what we were doing, hoping to get the same kind of edge, and the pride that went along with it.

Push-Up Principle
You can't change people's basic qualities; accept them the way they are.

One of the primary mistakes managers make is trying to change people. They focus all their energy on a person's weakest area and try desperately to turn that weakness into a strength. I am here to tell you that you can't do it. Everybody has his or her strengths and weaknesses. You've got to focus on a person's strengths, and build on them. Everybody has at least one area in which he's really special. Find that area of strength and build on it, and forget the weakness.

You can look for negatives, or you can look for positives. And until you develop the ability to look for positives, you can't build a productive relationship. Looking for negatives builds an attitude of criticism and disapproval.

You can't just "pick out positives" occasionally. You must do it consistently, every day, all the time, until it becomes a way of life. It can't be a part-time commitment.

Push-Up Principle
Always look for reasons to praise.

The real key to praise is that it's got to be spontaneous. You can't just say, "Well, I'm going to praise that guy once a week." You must really look for a genuine reason to praise him. Don't worry about overdoing it. You can't praise your people, or love your people, too much. Always have a good word for people every time you see them, and let them know whenever you notice something they've done well.

In a sense, you've got to become a good-will ambassador. Always be the person who's saying something good about somebody. I know that it can be a challenge. Sometimes, you have to look pretty hard to find something to praise. But it's there, somewhere, because everybody has good qualities.

The most important thing is that it's got to be natural. It's got to be sincere and come from the heart. If you really love people, and care about them, you won't build a phony kind of relationship.

Push-Up Principle
Be slow to criticize.

When you work with people one-on-one, you can say 99 positive things and one negative thing, and the only thing they'll remember is the negative. Your emphasis has got to be positive. You've got to lift their strengths. You must be slow to criticize. I know you are thinking, "Isn't there any action I can take when someone is doing badly? Can I just let it slide?"

I believe the most acceptable form of punishment is lack of praise.

I believe that this method is 10 times more powerful than criticism. If you withhold praise, you let the person know that he's not one of the leaders. If you're someone who constantly gives praise, he'll know he's doing poorly when you stop praising, just as much as he would if you criticized him. You've let him know that he's not on the winning team right now, yet you haven't berated him or said anything negative.

When you want to criticize, don't. Spend your time making heroes out of other people. Give the people who are doing the job more love and attention. Before you know it, the poor performer will be dying to get back into the group that's getting praise and respect, and he'll improve his performance to do so. You'll accomplish the same end without saying anything hurtful.

When you only single out poor performance, you make people feel rotten. They're so down on themselves that they won't do anything. All you accomplish is convincing them that they can't do anything right, so there's no reason to try. And that's not what you wanted at all.

We all know, however, that there are times when you must address a problem directly. How can you give constructive criticism without bringing up individual failures? I believe the best time to discuss a "negative" is in a group setting. When several people are present, you can address problems without singling out any individual for criticism. Even though your problem won't apply to all the people in the group, you can get your point across without embarrassing the person who is guilty of the problem.

At the same time, you can single out individuals who have handled a situation well, put them in the spotlight, and let everyone see the kind of action that inspires praise and recognition.

One of my managers tells me that I sometimes use a method he calls the "hint and motivate" method. I simply "hint" at the problem, without directly criticizing people, then tell them about my confidence in them and the good things they've done. The "hint and motivate" method is another indirect way to point out a problem without causing discouragement and negative feelings.

Push-Up Principle
Don't hide your praise under a basket. Praise in public as well as in private.

When you want to praise someone for something he's done right, it's great to tell that person, but even greater if you tell him in front of other people. To the person you're praising, it's even more pleasant, and to the people listening, it's motivation to do what it takes to get praise for themselves.

Public recognition is a principle that I live by in my business. Every meeting and convention has time set aside for recognizing people who have turned in a great performance, either in sales or management or whatever. And don't just talk. Give people some memento of your recognition, like a plaque or certificate. But remember, it's not the cost or size of the award that counts. It's the recognition. People love being singled out as someone special.

When I first founded my company, I wanted to reward people who were doing well, but I could only reward a few because I couldn't afford enough engraved plaques to award everyone who was doing well. One day it came to me. I would give "t-shirt awards," just like I had given to the high school football players when I was coaching. My wife couldn't believe it. "Art," she said, "you can't give grown-ups t-shirt awards. They'll think you've gone nuts." Well, Angela is right 99 percent of the time, but I just had a feeling about those shirts. I presented my first "t-shirt awards" at our next company meeting, and the people loved them. The slogans were simple, and some were funny, but they had powerful messages — things like "I Ain't Average," "I Am A Stud," and "I Am Somebody." Today, over seven years and a lot of success later, I give lots of different awards. But the t-shirt awards are still the most popular...and the most fun.

Recognition doesn't have to be an elaborate thing, either. It can be as simple as a hand-written note to say, "You're doing great. I am proud of you," or a phone call to say, "Congratulations, I am so glad you're on my team."

Several leaders in our company have told me that things really got going in their organizations when they started publishing a "leaders sheet" for their individual organizations, something we've done for years as a company. There's something

about seeing your name in print that motivates like nothing else.
I've seen people in our company who are already millionaires just
go crazy because they fell one slot lower than last month on the
leaders sheet! You'd think financial independence would
eliminate the need for recognition, but it doesn't. The more
praise and recognition people get, the more they want, and the
harder they will work to get it, whether they are making $100 or
$10,000 a month. As a leader, you can't lose with praise and
recognition. The results can't be anything but positive. There's
really nothing you do as a leader that's more important or will
help your people more than letting them know that you think
they are special and have great potential.

A great leader understands that it's much more important
for his people to receive recognition than for him to receive it.
When I got my first head football coach's job, my high school
coach called me one day and said, "Art, don't you ever forget
this. A great head coach always gives his assistant coaches and
players credit when the team wins. Don't ever miss an
opportunity when you're talking to the press to give them
recognition for the victory. But, also remember that the head
coach always takes all the blame when you lose."

That's good advice to apply to your business, too. When
your company or your department does something special, give
all the praise and all the credit to your people. You will get your
share of recognition for any job well-done because you're the
leader. But your people may be overlooked unless you point out
their contributions. That lets them know that you're working for
their success, as well as your own. A great leader will never let his
people think they are working just to help him get a promotion
or make big money. People must see you as working to help
them.

A Few Keys to Successful Recognition
1. Say something special about each award. Spend a few
   moments talking about the person, his sacrifice and his
   achievements before presenting the award. *Never* hand out a
   plaque with only a handshake, even if the meeting lasts until 2
   a.m.
2. Always recognize 20-25 percent of the crowd. If you have 20

people at a meeting, give five awards. If you have 300 people, give 75 awards.

3. Try to think of different kinds of awards. I once had a person who accomplished something truly great. I wanted to do something special and completely different. He was six feet tall, so I had a six-foot trophy made for him. Think of different names for your plaques and t-shirts — I use such things as "The Perfect Leader," "I Am A Champion," "Our Greatest," and so on.

4. Have fun. Make recognition entertaining, and the highlight of every meeting.

5. Always include the spouses. Put both the husband and wife's name on the plaques. Have the spouse come on stage to accept the award along with the winner. Promote "the team." Have special awards that honor the spouse's contributions, things like "Most Supportive Partner."

6. People who "slip back a little" deserve recognition, too. I give the "Torn Sweater" award, the "I Almost Made It" award, the "Flash in the Pan" award, and the like. This can be a funny way of reminding someone who usually does well or has great potential that you know he can do much better.

   But remember, never give this kind of award unless the person has fantastic ability and you know he will use the award as a challenge — a positive kind of "kick in the behind."

7. You can never give too much recognition, as long as it's sincere and from the heart. I know one superstar leader who gives the "Manager of the Day" award!

Start practicing the art of sincere praise and recognition. You'll be amazed at what your people can do...and even more amazed at how much they want to do it!

Chapter 5

The Forgotten Power

Management Mistake

Most businesses underestimate the role of the spouse in their people's success.

Leadership Solution

Leaders who involve the spouse build both business and personal success.

While we're on the subject of recognition, let's pause a minute here to talk about a type of recognition that's tremendously important but often overlooked. I'm talking about recognition of the role of the spouse in a person's business success.

I think it's accurate to say that, in most cases, a person's spouse usually has more influence than anyone else in his life. Yet, it seems that, in most businesses, the spouse falls under the heading of "personal life," and traditional business people believe that personal life and business don't mix.

Most businesses refuse to employ a husband and wife in the same company, even if they do entirely different jobs. In some organizations, if two single employees meet at work and decide to marry, one of them must resign.

Traditionally, the only place spouses are recognized is at a few social events throughout the year, or at the occasional convention, where they are expected to sit in their rooms or around the pool until the business meetings are over.

I believe that leaders who exclude their own spouse, and the spouses of their people, are ignoring an area that offers tremendous opportunities for pushing up people.

Push-Up Principle

Recognize, believe in, and commit to the importance of the supportive spouse.

I can speak about this from experience. From our earliest days together, my wife, Angela, has always been an equal partner in my work life. We didn't think of work as something I did alone. Even when our two children were small, Angela always took an active interest in my work, and participated in many ways. She was always super-supportive. I always recognized the importance of a positive, supportive spouse and encouraged the other spouses one-on-one when our company was small. But as the company grew, we were doing very little to address the spouses as a group and to recognize the contributions they made.

For some time, I had tried to get Angela to speak to spouses at some of our meetings, but she was very nervous about speaking before a large group.

Finally, at one of our conventions, I called the spouses together as a group and talked to them about the importance of spouse support and paying the price for success. I did this for two years at our annual convention. The second year, at the end of the speech, one of the manager's wives spoke up from the back of the room. Her husband had been in the business for a couple of years, and seemed to be working hard, but he was still struggling. In the sales business, living on commission income can be tough while you're learning the business. He and his wife had two small children, and they were having financial problems.

Her words hit me hard. "Art," she said "you always talk about 'paying the price, paying the price.' I'm willing to do anything. I'm willing to pay any price. But what is my price? Just tell me what it is and I'll pay it." Her desperation just devastated me. For once in my life, I was speechless!

For the first time, it dawned on me that the spouses' problems were not the same as the managers'. They had a totally unique set of concerns.

Angela realized it, too. She could identify with these people. She knew much better than I did that being married to a salesman and living on a commission income was no easy life. She had struggled herself before learning how to cope with it.

The following year at the convention, we again set aside special time for a spouse meeting. But this time, Angela got up, very nervously, and spoke to the group about her personal experiences, and how she had overcome some specific problems.

From that time on, we recognized the spouses as an active part of our company, not only by including them and encouraging them to participate in all our meetings, but also by arranging meetings especially for them. Angela travels with me wherever I go, speaking, communicating and encouraging the spouses.

Today, our company has an active spouse group, which contains both male and female spouses, called the "Partners Organization." Every convention or seminar agenda includes a packed schedule of Partners meetings; a monthly newsletter keeps the group informed; the Partners have their own special projects that help support the activity of their spouses. We do this as a company, but we encourage it on a local level, as well. Most important, spouses are invited to attend any management meeting that their partner attends. It's wonderful to see our company leaders, all the way up to top sales directors, at these meetings with their partners sitting alongside them. I firmly believe that spouse support is a major ingredient in the tremendous individual success our people have had to date.

Push-Up Principle

Two people who are united in life, working toward the same goals and dreams, can achieve more than one person.

It's a fact that your people's spouses will have an effect on their business life, one way or the other. If the spouse understands and supports the business goals of the partner, and works actively toward achieving those goals, the positive effects are incredibly powerful. The person with a supportive spouse has a more positive attitude, a stronger commitment to work, and higher self-esteem and confidence. There is a sense of shared dreams and goals, a feeling of going in the same direction. The business has double power, with two people working toward business success instead of just one.

Supportive spouses will apply whatever talents they have to their partners' business goals, and be more willing to overlook the frustrations and focus on the future potential. The spouse is a main source of motivation for any individual. An excited, enthusiastic partner can motivate a person to excel far more than any supervisor.

On the other hand, a negative, unsupportive spouse can be a disaster to a promising business career. If the spouse's opposition or disapproval is causing friction and conflict, there's no way that the person can come into work each day feeling fresh and ready to give it his best shot. Attitude, activity, self-esteem, and commitment are affected. If you are the kind of leader who is interested in people as individuals, you just can't overlook this type of emotional conflict.

There are many reasons why a person's career can cause conflict at home. In many cases, the more successful a person becomes in business, the less happy the spouse becomes. Often, it's because the business person has developed more, moved ahead more, and grown in confidence more than the spouse.

The more successful a person becomes, the more highly driven and ambitious one may become. One may be even more preoccupied with work, and have less personal time for the family. The gap between the person's business and family worlds widens, and the couple may have trouble finding common ground and time for communication. The spouse may feel isolated and frustrated, because less and less is shared between the two. Sharing a business life can eliminate this problem, and increase the bond between husband and wife.

Push-Up Principle

Reward the contributions that the spouses make to the success of their partner and the company.

As I mentioned earlier, you can highlight the contributions that spouses make in the same ways that you recognize the accomplishments of your people. Plaques, certificates, or t-shirt awards could work great as spouse awards, too. Include a special spouse section in all of your awards banquets and meetings. Recognize the contribution that a supportive spouse makes to the business, and make the spouse feel that his or her contribution is appreciated, not just by the partner, but by the whole company.

Encouraging spouse involvement in your business takes a little effort, but it's worth it. As a leader, you must be interested in production, profits, and the bottom line. But you don't want your company to have great success "in spite of" its effect on the personal lives of your people.

The good results of pushing up spouses far outweigh the effort. To be totally effective, the "forgotten member" of the team needs to be remembered, and recognized for the contribution he or she can make. You know the positive effects of a team spirit in your business. Remember that a team spirit at home is the foundation of business success.

Chapter 6

Freedom With Responsibility

Management Mistake

Most managers over-supervise, denying employees responsibility and the freedom to work independently.

Leadership Solution

Leaders know that freedom and responsibility are critical to their people's growth and development.

One of the best kinds of recognition you can give your people is to recognize their worth to you and to your business. And the best way to acknowledge that worth, and your faith and trust in them, is by giving them the two qualities most valued by people in any job — freedom and repsonsibility.

The concept of "freedom with responsibility" is one of the basic principles of the free enterprise system. You take good people who want to be "somebody," give them responsibility and allow them to handle that responsibility on their own. Then, you reward them according to their level of achievement.

That's the way this country was built, and it works just as well today as it has in the past. The people who perform, who accomplish something, are rewarded for their efforts with recognition and financial success.

Somewhere along the way, we sort of lost sight of that basic principle in American business. In so many traditional companies, people are given very little responsibility or freedom. There are so many levels of authority and so much struggling for power and position that most people just get lost in the shuffle. Everybody has duties, but you have to be at the highest management levels before you have any responsibility. Often, who you know, not what you know, has as much to do with being promoted and recognized as how you perform.

Push-Up Principle

People need to know that individual initiative will be recognized and rewarded.

The freedom with responsibility concept is one of the main differences between the free enterprise system and the communist and socialist systems. In those systems, everybody works for the state. Individual performance means very little. Regardless of how you perform, you eat the same as everybody else, and you get the same kinds of rewards as everyone else.

Many companies in America today have become socialistic in their thinking. They put people in little cubicles, give them a few tasks to do, and then check on them all the time. One guy does a great job for the company, the guy behind him does a terrible job, and both get the same "across the board" raise. Their manager doesn't judge the quality of their work individually. This situation can be very frustrating, because they feel that the manager doesn't take into account their particular talents and abilities. People need constant feedback about their work in order to improve and grow, and you should be the one to provide that feedback, person-to-person.

Feedback is important, too, in helping people understand their role in the company or business. Often, employees have little knowledge of "the big picture." Because many managers don't share the goals and strategies of the company with their people, most don't know how their specific job contributes to the company's overall objectives or how it benefits those who use the company's products or services. If you don't involve people in what's happening around them, they won't feel that you recognize their worth or their contribution.

I believe that these are major reasons for discontent among people in the workplace today. If you ask ten people whether or not they like their jobs, nine will say no. Most of them will complain that they aren't recognized for their work or that they don't have enough responsibility.

When you hire people, you should have enough confidence in them to give them responsibility and increase that responsibility as their performance warrants it. People will go out there and really "bust it" if you give them the authority and freedom to do the job on their own.

Push-Up Principle

People need to feel a sense of ownership toward the job they do.

A lot of the freedom with responsibility theory has to do with the concept of ownership. Whether it's ownership of your own business, or ownership of the duties you perform for a company, that concept is critical to every individual who takes pride in his work. People need to have work that belongs to them, and know that they will be evaluated on how they handle that work.

My daddy was a great teacher, and he understood the concept of ownership. My folks didn't have a lot of money, and when I turned 16 and wanted to get a car, my daddy let me buy my own car with money I had earned.

I took care of that car like you wouldn't believe. I wouldn't let kids get in and spill milkshakes on the seats or leave trash in the car, because I had paid my hard-earned money for it. I didn't go out and "scratch-off" and burn the rubber off my tires, because I bought the dadgum tires.

That experience taught me a lesson I'll never forget. The car I bought was my car. I was free to do whatever I wanted with it, but I was also responsible for it. That built a sense of responsibility in me that I would never have had if my parents had just bought the car and handed me the keys. I believe that freedom with responsibility in business works the same way.

Push-Up Principle
A leader recognizes the basic freedoms that most people want in their work environment.

What are the freedoms that people are looking for in business? They're simple things, like the freedom to be your own boss and the freedom to control your own destiny. We all want to feel that we have some control over our income, and to know that we'll get compensated for the effort we put in. We need the freedom to make our own decisions, and, most important, the freedom to succeed or fail on the basis of our own efforts. We all want the freedom to dream our own dreams, and to be able to work toward those dreams.

Chances are the people who work with you are no different from anyone else. It's important that you, as a leader, recognize those basic freedoms and create an environment where those freedoms are possible.

Push-Up Principle
Freedom is only possible when it goes hand-in-hand with responsibility.

Responsibility is the other side of freedom. You can't talk about one without the other, because the two concepts must go hand-in-hand in order to work effectively. Unfortunately, this is the part that many people don't understand. Often, people want the freedom to do things their way, but don't want to take the responsibility for their actions.

During the last few years in this country, we've developed an emphasis on selfishness. There's even been a name coined for people growing up in the last decade — the "me" generation. Sometimes it seems that everybody is concerned with what the other person can do for them. You know how it goes, "Give me my freedom, give me my rights, give me everything." But the problem is that often people don't want to put anything back in. They don't take the time to consider other people's rights and freedoms. All they want to know is, "What can I get out of this country? What can I get out of this job? What's in it for me?"

As a leader, you must help your people understand that there are responsibilities that go with basic freedoms. The price for those freedoms is work, commitment, fairness, and consideration of others. They have a responsibility to follow the basic rules of the company or organization. It can't be a one-way street. No one in any company can have unlimited freedom and no responsibility. People must be willing to take full responsibility for their work and the results of it.

Push-Up Principle
As a leader, you have the same freedoms and responsibilities as your people.

One of the advantages of leadership is the opportunity to do things *your way*. You have freedom to set your own goals, to decide on how you're going to achieve them, and to make decisions along the way. But, along with those freedoms comes the total responsibility for what happens. One of the challenges of leadership is that the heaviest responsibility falls on your shoulders, as well as the best rewards. What you and your people ultimately accomplish is your responsibility.

One of the toughest things for most leaders is to accept blame for mistakes and not make excuses. When things go wrong in your business, you've got to point the finger at yourself, not at anyone or anything else. So many times, when there's a problem, your first impulse is to say, "The competition caused this," or, "It's John's fault that this happened."

The famous running back, O.J. Simpson, realized the error of making excuses. He said, "I believe the day you take complete responsibility for yourself, the day you stop making any excuses, is the day you start to the top." Simpson knew what he was talking about. The only thing you accomplish when you make excuses is to lose the respect of your people.

A strong leader has to be someone who can make a mistake, take responsibility for it, and do what it takes to make sure it's not repeated again. Only when you are able to do that can you expect to ask the same standards of responsibility of your people.

When I graduated from college and took my first job as an assistant coach, my head coach taught me a fantastic lesson. I showed up for the first coaching meeting, and I was so excited I couldn't stand it. It was a dream come true for me just to be there.

At the meeting, the head coach divided up the practice responsibilities, and we each took our group for 25 minutes of individual practice before we came together as a group. I was the backfield coach.

There I was, so young and fresh out of school. After we split up, I went to the head coach and said, "Coach, what do you want me to do with my group?" His answer surprised me. He said, "Art, I hired you to coach backs. Now, those backs are yours. I want them ready to play on Friday night. I didn't hire you to tell you what to do. You just get the job done, OK?"

That lesson has stuck with me all through my business life. When you give people a job to do, let them do their job. Don't tell them how you would do it. The only way to test ability is to put your people out on the field and let them play. Let them have the freedom and the responsibility to win or lose. Your job is to give them support and encouragement. If you only ask them to imitate you, you'll never know what they could really do on their own — and neither will they.

PART II

Basic Principles To Master In Developing Leaders

It is commonly said that "salesmen aren't born; they're made." The same is true of leaders!

Traditional companies think in terms of going out and searching for people to fill key management positions. At A.L. Williams, we believe in building and developing leaders from within the company. We feel that if we are good enough to build a company, we are good enough to run it.

In most companies, there are only a few positions at the top. Leaders who hold these positions have a tendency to covet their position and hold others back for their own self-interest. In our company, people are paid for producing leaders. The more leaders they produce who are successful, the more personal success they have.

We believe that the more leaders a company builds, the further that company can go in the business world. People will have a greater sense of loyalty and commitment to the company if there success and opportunity have come as a result of being pushed up and promoted within the company.

The principles in these next chapters reflect the value of "pushing up" leaders. It's to any leader's advantage to master these principles, to teach and instill these principles in others — and to push up leaders in abundance.

Chapter 7

Stand For Something

Management Mistake

*Many managers change their principles
to suit their business.*

Leadership Solution

*Leaders have the highest principles in both their
business and personal life.*

In business, does the bottom line justify everything? I've heard people say that doing what's right in your personal and community life is one thing, but those kinds of "old fashioned" principles just don't apply in the "dog-eat-dog" world of business. I don't agree.

I believe that doing what's right is just as important in business as it is in your personal life. People tell me that just doing what's right in business isn't good enough. But there's no substitute, in my book, for providing a real service to people that's based on sound principles and backed by a committed group of people.

As a leader, this is a critical area. If you want people to follow your lead, if you want to establish an atmosphere of teamwork and shared goals, you've got to have some principles, and you've got to be prepared to stand by them. There is nothing that will disillusion people more quickly than a leader who is wishy-washy and unprincipled.

Today, it's hard to find anybody who will take a position. People have lost faith with politicians, as a rule, because they say one thing one day and something else the next. If they provoke a little opposition, they'll change their position overnight. Everybody has a feeling that politicians are going to say whatever they have to say to get a vote. And these are supposedly the leaders of our country! People have become so disenchanted that they won't support any candidate; they just take a passive attitude about the whole subject.

The same thing happens in business. People just won't believe in a manager or a company that's not doing what's right for its customer or client. Companies sell whatever makes a buck, a little bit of this and a little bit of that. Managers follow that "bottom line" philosophy, and the employees sense it.

Push-Up Principle
In business, reputation is everything.

People can smell a phony a mile away. When a salesman goes out to sell a product, the client isn't buying the company that the salesman represents. The client is buying the salesman. To that client, the particular salesman who calls on him IS the company. Often, his decision to buy is based as much on his trust in the salesman as it is on the product itself.

The same thing applies when you hire a new person in your company. To that person, YOU are the influencing factor. In most cases, people don't join your company because they trusted the company; they joined because they trusted YOU.

It's quite a responsibility, when you stop and think about it. In truth, it just may be the biggest responsibility you'll ever have.

You can't fool people for very long. What you do as a leader had better be right, because your reputation is at stake with every decision you make. If you're not right in your principles and objectives, you might get by for one day or one week or one year, but sooner or later, people are going to find you out. The result can be embarrassment and a ruined reputation. One person talks to another, and soon you're out of business.

You've got to strive to be right — ethically and in practice — 100 percent of the time. You can't go out and start a business, hire people who are depending on you, and then hope to find out in six months or six years that what you were doing was good for customers and your people. You've got to *know* it's right from the very beginning. If you don't, you're in the wrong business.

As a manager, your people put it on the line for you every day. Every day they *assume* that you are doing what's right, that you are keeping your promises and providing leadership with their best interests in mind.

Push-Up Principle

Trust and respect buy a loyalty that you can never buy with salary.

Everyone needs someone and something to believe in. As adults, most people have learned the hard way that many people are only out for themselves. They have discovered, often through a hurtful process, that many people just can't be trusted. You'd think everyone would be jaded; but the truth is, past hurts make most people more appreciative of someone who's trying to do right. If you can develop your people's trust in you, they'll return the favor with a loyalty and devotion that you just can't buy with salary. They'll give you 150 percent every time if they think you're going to give them a fair deal. On the other hand, if they think you have no principles, you don't "stand" for anything, no amount of money can buy their best efforts.

If you want your people to succeed, you've got to give them an example of fairness and honesty, above any example you set in the areas of knowledge or technical expertise. They can admire your business savvy and your personal success, and that's important. But if they think you will stab them in the back if it's to your advantage, they will never respect you or make their best efforts for you.

Push-Up Principle
Before you can become a great leader, you've got to become a great person.

One of the great NFL fullbacks, Earl Campbell, said a lot when he shared his "secret" to greatness. "Somebody will always break your records," he said. "It's how you live that counts."

How true! Your people aren't going to accept your leadership just because of your position. I've always reminded people in our company that, "A position doesn't make a person, a person makes a position." As a leader, you're judged, first and foremost, by the kind of person you are, deep down. Regardless of how good you are in business, people see you *first* as a person. Your morals, your position in your town or community, your relationship with your family...everything you are counts. If you are going to "push people up," they've got to be convinced that you have something valuable to offer. They've got to want to follow your lead in order for you to help them.

I believe that, before you can become a great leader, you've got to become a great person. When I say great, I'm talking about real character — things like honesty, integrity, loyalty, sincerity. Character is so important, because it's the foundation that you'll build everything else in your life around.

Back in 1977, when we started our company, it was almost unheard of for a company to sell the type of product that we sold, and even worse not to diversify into a lot of different products. But we sold what we believed in — and nothing else. Now, you might not buy our product, and you might not come to work with our company, but you darn sure know were we stand *all the time*.

It's important that your people understand what you're trying to accomplish, and be able to see exactly where you stand. They must know that you're not going to switch over and support something else tomorrow or a week from now. Only if they know your commitment is total can you gain their commitment and their efforts.

If you're having problems getting people to follow your lead, it could be that your reputation among your own people isn't all that it could be. Put your principles first, and let everyone in your business know that those principles are important to you.

Stand for something — and you'll find that people want to follow you, because you're the kind of person they're proud to call their leader.

Chapter 8

Total Commitment Is The First Step To Greatness

Management Mistake

Some managers have only a half-hearted commitment to what they're doing, and it shows.

Leadership Solution

A great leader has a total commitment to his business and personal goals.

In every person's life, there are many important moments. But in your business life, there's one moment that stands out from all the others. It's the moment that you take the first step to greatness, when you change from someone with a job to someone with a purpose. I'm referring to the moment that you decide to make a total commitment to your goals.

Push-Up Principle
You can't ever be truly successful until you make a total commitment.

People have difficulty making a commitment to anything. They spend their whole lives going from one thing to another, looking for a quick and easy way to success, or else they just settle for something less than their dreams. Many people make a half-hearted commitment to something, and tell themselves they are making a total commitment. Then they see something better somewhere else; the grass looks greener in a new business or job. They commit for a little while to something new. Then they get tired of that business, too, and they're off again to something else.

Now, I don't believe that you have just one chance to do something great in your life, but I don't believe that you get an unlimited number of chances, either. Sometime in your life, you've got to stop running. You've got to say, "Now, this is it. This is a good opportunity and I'm going to take it all the way. This time, I'm going to stand and fight until I win."

When you finally make that total commitment, nothing in your life will be the same. Maybe for the first time, you'll have a real direction in your life, a purpose for getting up in the morning and working hard every day. When you see everything you do as one more step toward reaching the goals you've committed to, no task seems too big or too small.

Push-Up Principle
Total commitment helps develop mental toughness.

One of the best benefits of total commitment is that it helps you to develop the mental toughness you need to withstand the pressures that build up in any area of work. When you've made the decision to make your business or organization work, no matter how hard you have to work, no matter what comes up, you eliminate the possibility of quitting. It's amazing how you learn to take problems and turn them into opportunities to improve your business and yourself instead of using them as excuses for your failure. And, it's amazing how you learn to rise to the occasion and find solutions to problems when you've committed to win "no matter what."

Push-Up Principle
Successful people do what it takes, and a little bit more.

As I talk to salespeople across the country, I'm often asked what I think makes the difference between being good at what you do and being great. I've had plenty of chances to observe successful people at all levels, and I've got a theory about that. Our company has two sales managers in the Midwest who, on the surface, look the same — same age, same sex, same city, same position, etc. One is good at what he does and makes $50,000 a year. The other is also good at what he does and makes $500,000 a year.

What's the difference between them? I believe it's the "little bit more" principle. The guy who makes $500,000 works hard...and a little bit more. He knows how to build successful people in his organization...and a little bit more. He goes out there and produces every day...and a little bit more. He's got a will to win...and a little bit more.

The person who really wins big, financially and in terms of success and recognition, always does everything that's required of him, everything it takes to win, and then he goes on and does just a little bit more than what's required.

I believe that total commitment is the secret behind that ability. When you're totally committed to what you're doing, you've got that extra "plus" that it takes to keep going when you get tired and want to stop.

There's a leader in our company that I like to talk about because he exemplifies the "little bit more" principle. He's an incredible executive, admired for his outstanding ability by everyone in the company. He's broken all the company records over and over, and even set the amazing record of earning over $100,000 in one month!

Now, this guy is financially independent many times over. He's in his early 40s, and he's done so well that there's no real reason for him to work. But he does work. He has a huge sales organization with offices all across the country. He works hard all day at his business, and that should be enough. But that's not all he does. Every few nights, after his regular work day is over, he picks up the telephone, tired from an already full day, and begins to call his people across the country, checking on their progress, encouraging them, just "touching base" or helping them with a problem. A few hours later, long after everyone else has left the office, he goes home.

This guy does all he's supposed to...and a little bit more. That's part of the secret of his success. For him, it's become a way of life, and it's served him well in his career. That willingness to keep going for a few hours after most of the business world has "called it a day," has meant the difference between a good, solid career and overwhelming success.

It's not easy to go back to work when the rest of the world is going home to watch TV. That's where total commitment comes in. Only if you have that commitment, and the mental toughness that grows from it, can you keep up the determination and endurance that it takes to win.

Push-Up Principle

Before you can be totally committed, you've got to love and believe in what you are doing.

Trying to improve yourself, helping your people and dealing with competition takes energy and drive. The path to success is spelled W-O-R-K. I believe you'll never be able to put in the long hours and face the tough challenges if you don't love what you do. Few people have ever succeeded in an area that they had no interest in. Behind all the great success stories of American business is a strong belief in the worth of the task, and a plain old love of the job.

When I was teaching and coaching football in south Georgia, there was an English teacher that I ate lunch with sometimes. Whenever I saw her, she was always upset about how badly her students were doing in English. "Art, I can't get them to pay attention at all," she'd say. "They don't do their homework, they won't listen in class, they don't even make the slightest effort. I just don't know what's wrong with these kids! I can't understand why they hate English so much!"

One day I got to thinking about her problem and the difference in the way the kids acted in English and on the football field. The kids she was talking about were many of the same kids who voluntarily came out to football practice every afternoon and sweated and rolled around in the dirt and just killed themselves. Nobody was making them do it, and they weren't even getting any school credit for it! They made a tremendous effort every day, and they had a great attitude.

I began to wonder if part of my friend's problem could be that *she* didn't love what she was doing as much as she should. Maybe she wasn't communicating the excitement and enthusiasm of someone who thinks English is the greatest thing in the world. I wondered what would happen if she jumped up in her chair or threw an eraser up in the air when she got fired up about something in a short story or a play, like we did in football practice when something went well. By being so formal with her class and not showing them how much she loved English, maybe she had failed to convince them that English was fun and exciting, and that they could love it, too.

I believe that there's no substitute for loving what you do. It's the ingredient around which your entire commitment is based. When great athletes are asked about all the time and effort they've put into their sport over the years, they're likely to talk about love of their sport. Baseball great Mickey Mantle was one such athlete. "To play ball was all I lived for. I used to like to play so much that I loved to take infield practice. Hitting — I could do all day. I couldn't wait to go to the ballpark. I hated it when we got rained out."

The important point here is that there's more to commitment than how much money you think you can make or how fast you think you can succeed. Those things are important, of course, but those things alone rarely provide the motivation that it takes to weather the bad times and to keep going after it day after day after day. Love and pride in what you do adds a new dimension to your commitment. And, it's been my experience that when people love what they do, success comes more easily, and more naturally, than it would ever have come if they were slugging away at something they really hated.

Total commitment is something you must help build and encourage in your people, too. You can't make people love their job, but you can show them the positive things they are doing, and involve them in such a way that they feel a part of the overall operation.

As a leader, your personal commitment is passed on to your people. When you become totally committed to your business or organization, you won't have to announce it to your people; they will be able to tell. Nothing excites people more than being around someone who has a purpose and a goal. When it comes to leading by example, you can't do anything more important than set an example of total commitment to your work. Follow-the-leader is more than just a game. It's a reality in the business world, where people look to their manager to find a pattern for their own business lives.

Everybody wants to follow a man or woman who's committed to what they do. Every election year, unpaid volunteers spend countless hours working for candidates simply because they want to be a part of an organization led by a committed person. They're attracted by someone who seems to know where he's going and is totally devoted to his goals.

Committed people attract other people like magnets. When they walk into a room, it just seems to light up. Your people in business want to feel that same kind of excitement and dedication; but they must see it in you first. Be an example of total commitment, and you won't have to go looking for committed people to bring into your business. They'll come to you.

Chapter 9

Become A Crusader

Management Mistake

Many managers are only in business to make a living.

Leadership Solution

*Leaders find a cause they believe in
and commit to it totally.*

One reason that it's so difficult for many people to make the kind of commitment necessary to win in business is that the only purpose of their business life is to earn a living. There's nothing wrong with that in itself. After all, we all have a responsibility to take care of ourselves and our families. But being in business for that purpose alone can be a pretty dry, unrewarding experience. You can see it expressed in the people who drag themselves to work every Monday and start counting the hours till Friday afternoon.

One trait that I've noticed in people who have made giant strides in the business world is that they have a special outlook on their work. They don't look at it as work! Many of them don't know when their work day starts and when it ends. They rarely take vacations, because they aren't looking for a way to get away from their jobs — they love their jobs.

It's not the same as being a "workaholic," someone who has nothing in his life but his job. It's simply that, to these lucky people, work is not a burden to be endured. It's fun.

I understand this feeling, because I've had it myself for the past seven years. I experienced the change from someone who "had to work" to someone who "loved to work." And I know the reason for it, at least in my own life.

My "job" changed when my attitude about what I was doing changed.

Push-Up Principle
Commit to something bigger than your business.

I'm convinced that a major reason our company has been so successful is that it was built around a passionate belief in a certain concept and a product that fit that concept. We felt that, due to reasons of self-interest among companies in our industry, the American consumer had not been introduced to a product and philosophy that we believed would serve them much better than the conventional products on the market.

That belief was the foundation of our business. Long before we knew when and where and how we were going to do it, we were determined to introduce the concept to consumers. We were so totally convinced that what we were doing was right that no amount of difficulty could discourage us. We were committed to our philosophy, in spite of the fact that it was totally at odds with what 95 percent of our industry was doing. We knew the opposition to our plan would be fierce.

We did meet opposition, but it only intensified our determination to crusade for what we believed was right. We developed a "crusading spirit" that was so intense it was like a passion. There was a lot to discourage us, and some difficult times, but there was also an element of excitement that I'd never experienced.

We couldn't wait to get to work in the morning. All we wanted to talk about were the plans for our company, and how we could make them a reality. Everyone got involved, and there was an explosion of creative thinking about how to achieve our goals that extended beyond the original people, involving their spouses, the secretaries in the office, even our children.

Whenever someone new joined the company, they seemed to "catch" the spirit of what we were doing almost immediately. All the people in the company went out and talked to everyone they met about what we were doing. Seven years later, that same spirit is still alive among the people in our company.

I firmly believe that we could never have gotten where we are today without believing in something more than just building a successful company. Sure, we were motivated to succeed, and we might have built a respectable business without having a specific "cause" as our cornerstone. But I think it would have been much less than the company we have today. There just wouldn't have been the same inspiration.

Your career can mean so much more to you if it's based on something more than just personal gain. To be really successful, I believe you've got to see yourself as an active participant in some great event. The time you spend at work is a large part of your life; I believe that a person's happiness at work depends on whether or not he feels that he's spending that time at something that will make a difference, something that, in his mind, is really worth doing.

Push-Up Principle

A crusading spirit provides the motivation and inspiration that inspires activity.

Crusaders die hard. Becoming a crusader will give you and your people the motivation, endurance and courage to "keep on keeping on" when times get rough. That's the thing that makes crusaders different from other managers and leaders. They have that extra edge that helps them continue in the face of tremendous adversity.

The kind of effort required to do something great with your life is more than most people can face without a total commitment to the principles behind their business. Only by being a crusader will you have that extra ounce of courage that will carry you through the difficult times until you win.

Push-Up Principle

Crusade for a cause that's worth the effort.

If you're going to become a crusader, it should go without saying that your cause must be something that's moral and right. It's got to be something that you really believe in — and it's got to be something that your people can believe in as well. You can't lead people if they think that the goals of your business are dishonest or even questionable. It comes right back to standing for something. Only by being right, and being 100 percent right, can you become a real crusader.

I know you must be thinking, "This all makes sense, but what about making money? Isn't that the reason we're out here in the business world to begin with?" Well, there's nothing wrong with making money, as long as you do a good job for people.

But I really believe that in order to make a lot of money, you've got to do what's right *first*. You've got to become a crusader *first*. When you commit to a significant cause and stick to it, I believe you have the advantage over the people who are just slugging it out for their paycheck.

Push-Up Principle
Crusaders learn to live with criticism.

The world is full of critics. The more you set out to do with your life, the more criticism you'll get. The people who sit around and do nothing are the only ones who can avoid being criticized. If you want to become a crusader, you'll have to learn to live with the comments and the actions of people who try to bring you down. The more innovative your cause, the more it goes against tradition, the more likely you are to be hit by a windfall of disapproval and complaints.

When I started out to do something different in my industry, I was totally unprepared for the negative reaction. It started with a lot of doomsaying. People said we were trying to do something impossible, and we were sure to fail. When we achieved a little success, things got rougher. There was a lot of name-calling, and a lot of half-truths and misinterpretations about our crusade. After our company began experiencing tremendous growth and acceptance by consumers, a few of our detractors really got vicious with their comments and their actions.

The first time I saw a newspaper article about our company, obviously written by someone who knew nothing about what we were trying to do, I was shocked. The first time I saw one that attacked me personally, I was devastated.

But, you know, the criticism only made us stronger. Once the sting of the words wore off, we were more determined than ever to succeed, to prove that what we were doing was right and could work.

That's the only way to deal with criticism. Instead of letting it bring you down, you have to take it as a challenge and get stronger from it, build on it. Always keep your purpose and your goals in front of you, and don't be swayed by what other people say. You've got to be true to yourself and your beliefs in business, just like you do in your personal life.

No one who's ever had a great cause has escaped the pain of criticism by those who were jealous of something new or didn't understand your purpose. If you're going to be a crusader, you must build on the strength of your convictions. You can never allow criticism to shake your determination to reach your goals. Ignore criticism and attacks when you can; when you can't ignore it, build on it and use it to strengthen your commitment.

Just remember the old saying, "What's popular isn't always right, and what's right isn't always popular!"

Push-Up Principle

Build your people's success by helping them to become crusaders.

One of the best things you can do for your people is to help them become crusaders. The best way to do that is to serve as an example of commitment, high principles, and crusading spirit. Your own devotion to and belief in your cause will be contagious. When people see your dedication, they'll be more likely to see their own work as more meaningful and less likely to see it as "just another job." Show them that you see them, not just as employees, but as a vital part of a crusade to help other people.

Remember, you are the leader; you are the example. The standards you set in service and performance are the standards that your people will have. You must be more committed, more devoted, and more convinced that you are doing what's right than anyone else.

When a new person comes to work with you, you've got to create that sense of involvement, not only in the operations of the business, but in the crusade. Then, and only then, will he be motivated to perform to his highest standards. Your commitment will be a step toward his commitment and an inspiration to be the very best he can be.

Push-Up Principle
Show people the good their efforts can accomplish.

One of the best ways to involve people in your company's crusade is to show them the good they can do. As a leader, there's little you can do that will have more impact on their careers and their future success than helping them to recognize the results of their work.

In the earliest days of our company, we had a young sales rep who was extremely carefree, almost irresponsible, and not very serious about our cause, his own future, or anything except having a good time.

Suddenly, a close relative died, leaving a wife and eight children with totally inadequate insurance protection. The situation was very serious, and brought our sales rep face-to-face with the cause our company was crusading for.

From that time on, he was a "madman" about bringing the company's crusade to average families like his own. In the small, traditional south Georgia town where he lived, opposition to his innovative program was strong. His automobile tires were slashed, and he was denied a bank loan he desperately needed because of the controversy surrounding his business. He and his wife suffered a lot of discomfort. But he never once waivered from his crusade; he just "put his shoulder to the wheel" and moved ahead.

This man probably wouldn't have made it with his original attitude toward his work. But once he knew the difference his work could make in someone's life, the crusade became a personal thing, and he approached his work with a seriousness he might never have had otherwise.

I see this happening all the time in our company. I get many letters from young members of our sales force who have had the same type of experience when delivering their first death claim. It's a sad and sobering experience, but for many people, it's the first time they've faced the real-life situations behind all the philosophy.

The rep may enter the client's home as his insurance representative, but he often leaves a crusader. For the first time in his career, he understands *why* he is working.

Show your people the good they can do. Show them how what they do each day translates into a needed service to people. For your people, the rewards will be increased dedication and pride. For you, as a leader, it will be the pleasure of working with a group of enthusiastic, committed people.

Find something you love and believe in, and become a crusader. Then, help your people to develop their crusading spirit. Once you do, you've practically assured your own success, and the success of your people.

Chapter 10

Develop A Positive Attitude

Management Mistake

Many managers dwell on their frustrations, disappointments and problems, and pass those negatives down to their people.

Leadership Solution

A leader always maintains a positive attitude, and passes that attitude to his people.

By now you may be saying to yourself, "Well, I want to treat people good and praise them. I want to become a crusader, and win the respect of my people. But, how can I accomplish all this? It's more than I can do!"

True, it is a tall order, especially if you're just getting started as a new leader. It's easy to get frustated and discouraged. But there's one quality that can give you the edge, that will help you to keep moving ahead. That quality is a positive attitude.

Attitude is an often-overlooked quality that has an unbelievable influence on success. I believe that you can do everything right in business, except have a positive attitude, and still fail. I really believe that attitude is everything. In fact, I believe the single most important thing you can accomplish in your lifetime is to develop a positive attitude.

Push-Up Principle

No one will follow a negative, dull, disillusioned, frustrated, dadgum crybaby.

They just won't do it. Negative people "drain your batteries." People like to be around people who are positive, confident, and excited.

We've all known people who are always groaning and moaning and complaining. After spending a few minutes with them, you feel like you're carrying around the weight of the world. You just feel miserable, and it makes you start thinking about your own problems.

What happens with those kinds of people? Little by little, you start to avoid them. When you see them coming, you just kind of walk in the other direction. You don't want to be dragged down by their negative attitude. That's exactly how people will feel about a leader with a negative attitude. Your people are looking to you for guidance and inspiration, and the last thing they want to hear from you is how bad everything is. They want to hear how great everything is, how excited you are about your business and how great you think their future is. People need to be excited and motivated, and no one was ever motivated by a "crybaby."

Push-Up Principle

Your business attitude is a reflection of the way you look at life.

A big part of your attitude depends on how you look at life in general. We're all here on this earth for a certain period of time. And we all start out in pretty much the same boat. Attitude has a lot to do with how we develop after that point.

So much of your actions depends on your attitude toward life. You can look at life two ways. You can look at life as a pain in the neck, or you can look at it as a beautiful, wonderful experience. It can be positive and exciting, or it can be a negative, disappointing experience. And *you* are the one who decides which way it is going to be. Your attitude will determine which road you take.

I made up my mind a few years ago that I was going to be as happy as possible, no matter what happened. I decided that I was tired of being frustrated and disappointed all the time. I decided that my life was going to be a great experience.

I am not saying it's easy to turn your attitude around. Many times it's tough, especially when you see so many negative things happening in the world around you. It's something that's totally self-made. A positive, winning attitude is not for sale. You can't buy it. You can't go to college and get it. It will only come when you make a total effort to look at life in a positive way, and practice it until it's second nature.

Stanley Beyer, a very successful man and a close personal friend of mine for years, is someone who knows first-hand about winning. In a speech he made to our company, he talked about maintaining a positive attitude. "People think that when you get to a successful position where you have money and recognition and success, everything is great and wonderful all the time. They think that we are positive all the time, that we don't have the same problems. But you know," Stanley said, "all the great people I have ever known have these same problems. They are positive only for a certain period of time.

"At first, you are confident and positive for maybe a few seconds, and then maybe you get negative. Then you become a little more successful, and you become positive for a few minutes, then for a few hours, then for a few days. The most confident, successful, positive person I have ever known was only that way for a short period of time. Everybody has fears and doubts. Everybody goes into depressions. The most successful people in the world doubt whether they can make it or not. But the only way you can handle that is by having a positive attitude, knowing that if you just hang in there long enough, things will work out."

How true! I am not trying to tell you that you just decide to have a positive attitude and it happens. Stanley's right. You've got to work at it every day, and soon you'll find yourself being positive a little more often, then a little more often than that.

There's a quote that I love, that's been helpful to me when I've been low and discouraged. It says that "Most people can stay motivated for two or three months. A few people can stay motivated for two or three years. But a winner can stay motivated for 30 years — or as long as it takes to win."

You won't become totally positive overnight, but you've got to keep working at it, keep building a winning attitude. I have a goal in my life. I'd like to have one 24-hour day — just one —when I didn't have one negative thought. I am probably one of the most positive guys you'll ever meet, and I can't go two or three hours without letting those negative thoughts creep in. I believe if you never had a negative thought, you would be the greatest person you could ever possibly be. It's so tough, but it's a goal to work toward every day. If you can just be positive most of the time, you'll be miles ahead of most other people.

Push-Up Principle
In your business, you must learn to pass negatives up and pass positives down.

This is a little saying that I introduced in our company a long time ago. It's a simple little guideline, but we've found that it works amazingly well.

It's simple in practice. Whatever your level in management, if you're having a problem or feeling really negative about something, find someone at your level or above to talk with. Talk freely with them. Get it out of your system. That way, when you go back to your people, you're not tempted to pass your disappointments and frustrations down to them. The manager you've talked with at a higher level is in a better position to cope with your negatives than the people who are looking to you for guidance and encouragement.

Many of our managers have actually set up this little agreement to be there for each other in bad times, so that each has a "safety valve" for letting off steam when problems just get to be too much. It works very well, because they understand that the frustrations are just temporary, and they're usually able to offer a little encouragement; and, the manager's people are never exposed to the kind of griping and complaining that might affect their own attitudes in a serious way.

Push-Up Principle

A bad attitude will cause failure faster than anything else.

Don't underestimate the power of attitude. Everything you accomplish in life, you accomplish through being positive. You don't accomplish anything long-lasting and great by being negative.

If you've got a winning attitude, you can slip up every day, in almost every way, and still win. You can be terrible at administration, green at selling, so scared you can hardly open your mouth, and still win. It's amazing but true. I've seen it happen a million times.

You can become fantastic in the technical aspects of your business, you can be the most learned guy in the world, the most creative guy, you can do everything right, but, if you don't have the ability to be positive in the face of disaster and bounce back, you'll never make it.

A positive attitude can have an incredible effect in your personal life, as well. It's OK to share some of your frustrations and disappointments with your spouse, but I'd hate to count the number of wives who see their husbands come in at night with scowls on their faces and then spend all evening complaining and moaning about what a rotten day they had. The husband sits there and sulks all night in front of the TV, then goes off the next morning with his scowl in place. It's a fact that a bad attitude can cause you to fail in your personal life, just like it can cause you to fail in business.

Boy, I can tell you that if you develop a positive attitude in your personal life, as well as your work life, you won't believe the positive results. Your spouse will be happy to see you come home at night, she'll enjoy being around you, and you'll see her own attitude (or his in the opposite case) make a tremendous change. It will bring a dimension of enthusiasm and positive feelings into your marriage and family life like you never believed possible.

Push-Up Principle

Let your people know that you expect them to work on developing a positive attitude.

As a leader, you must be available to help your people with their problems. You are the person that they must pass their negatives up to. You can expect some problems, and you should never discourage your people from approaching you with them.

But, there is a point where you must draw the line. You must be an example of a winning attitude yourself, and you must let your people know that you won't listen to just plain old griping and whining and complaining. You must encourage them to discuss their work problems with you, but you must be careful not to encourage complaints and negativism. When you meet with your people, deal with the problems, but never allow your meetings to become "gripe sessions." It's so easy for that to happen, especially if you're meeting with a large group. One negative remark leads to another, and the first thing you know everyone in the room is moaning and crying.

I have never used questionnaires in our business, because all the complaints and suggestions I receive come from the negative people and the non-producers. The positive people are appreciative, enthusiastic, and excited. Their mind is on going out and winning, not sitting down and thinking about mistakes and making criticisms and suggestions.

Make your people understand that you are there to help them with legitimate problems. But when it comes to plain old gripes, just give them a dose of encouragement. "I know you can work it all out, Joe," or "I know you won't let a minor thing like that stand in your way," are comments that show your support, but cut off Joe's opportunities to continue complaining. Always respond to minor complaints with a positive comment, and pretty soon folks will realize that you're not going to join in their complaint session. They will either find someone else who will listen, or they will be forced to give up their gripe sessions because they can see no one is interested in listening. If you lead an organization by example, and you build their confidence and help them develop a winning attitude, eventually gripes and complaints will sound so out of place in your group that they won't even come up.

Whenever someone in your group displays a positive attitude, praise him and let him know you appreciate it. Help him realize that it's the only path to being a winner, and that you see him that way.

Go out there every day with the desire to develop a winning attitude. Have a good feeling about yourself. See yourself doing something you're excited about. See yourself as somebody special. See yourself as a winner.

Chapter 11

You Get What You Expect

Management Mistake

Many people have low expectations of what they can accomplish.

Leadership Solution

Leaders expect to succeed, and they expect success for their people.

There's hardly anybody in America or the world who doesn't recognize Muhammad Ali as someone who always expected to succeed. He never kept it a secret. "I am the greatest," Ali said proudly. "Don't tell me I can't do something. Don't tell me it's impossible. Don't tell me I'm not the greatest, I'm the double greatest."

You may not want to encourage Ali's boastfulness in your people, yet everyone could benefit by his example of the refusal to accept the possibility of failure.

When people come to work with you in your business, they're standing on the edge of a new opportunity. Whether or not they succeed will depend on their expectations of themselves and on your expectations of them. This is an area where you have a tremendous opportunity to "push up" your people.

Push-Up Principle
Life gives people whatever they will accept.

I truly believe that life will give you whatever you will accept. If you accept failure, you will probably get failure. But if you expect to succeed, like Ali, you're much nearer to being a success. It's been proven over and over again that things will work out exactly as you see them working out in your life. If you accept being average and ordinary, life will make you average and ordinary. If you accept being poor, life will make you poor. If you accept being unhappy, life will give you that, too. But if you expect to be successful and happy — and won't accept anything less — chances are you will be.

It's sad to say, but I see so many people who don't expect to succeed. Maybe that's been their history; maybe they've tried two or three different things and none of them worked out. Maybe they think all companies are going to cheat them and hurt them because they've been cheated and hurt in the past. Many people are so down on themselves and their work experience that they've decided to expect the worst and save themselves from more disappointment. That kind of outlook will only inhibit success.

Push-Up Principle

A leader won't accept expectations of failure.

People are going to develop, in one direction or another, and it's your responsibility as a leader to help them develop in a positive way.

When I was coaching football, I believed in lots of weight training. I started noticing that, every Friday, when the boys went for their record weight for the week, they would try the lift a few times, then say, "I can't," and give up. All of a sudden, it seemed like all I heard was, "I can't." I started dreaming, "I can't." Finally I took action. I banned those two words from our team's vocabulary. I let the players and coaches know that I would not accept those words. We set a rule that if any player was caught saying, "I can't," the person who heard it would give the offender three licks with a paddle. I reminded them that we could do anything we wanted to do. I expected to win, and I wanted them to know that I expected them to be winners, too.

I don't know if it took two weeks or two months, but pretty soon our players and coaches stopped even thinking, "I can't." It was amazing how we immediately began to get better!

You may not be able to use that tactic with adults, but the principle is the same. You have to let your people know that, as a leader, you just won't tolerate that kind of thinking. Let them know that you *know* they can win, and you won't accept anything less than their best.

Push-Up Principle

People will rise to the standards you set for them.

Most people set certain standards for themselves. Unfortunately, these standards are usually too low. They don't have the confidence to set lofty standards, and they're afraid to risk failure.

You are more objective about your people's talents and potential than they are. You may be able to set goals for them that are still reachable, yet much higher than they'd ever set for themselves.

All of your people have talent; you know they can make a contribution or you wouldn't have put them on your "team" in the first place. Every time you set a goal and it's reached, you've helped build the confidence to reach for a higher goal. If you let people settle for modest goals, you'll wind up with average and ordinary people on your team instead of superstars.

You may be skeptical that your people will really believe you when you set high goals for them. How can they be expected to rise to *your* level of expectation? Anyone who's ever been coached at anything knows the answer. No individual will push himself as hard as he will with a coach. Many times, a coach is as responsible for an athlete's level of achievement as the athlete himself.

It's hard for people to push themselves to their limit with no one around to watch or encourage them. If Tom Landry told the Dallas Cowboys, "Guys, just go out there and practice by yourselves today," do you think the players would punish themselves and push themselves the same way they would with Landry calling advice and encouragement from the sidelines? As the leader, it's up to you to set the highest standard for achievement, what I call a "standard of excellence." Set it first with your own example, then set that same standard of excellence for your people, both individually and as a group.

Don't ever feel like your people's goals and standards of excellence are none of your business. They need a coach to push them forward, and they'll never resent the fact that you think they can do great things. The Dallas Cowboys may wish that Tom Landry would stay away from practice so they could take it easy, but you can bet they don't wish that on Super Bowl Sunday.

Push-Up Principle
Constant encouragement leads to increased expectations.

It may seem corny to keep telling people how great you feel about their potential, but don't worry. You can never encourage your people too much. That applies to new people just starting out and people who have been around for a long time. Nobody ever — and I mean *ever* — gets tired of being told that they're great and that you think they can do something really special.

Encouragement doesn't produce instant results. It may take months or a year of telling a person how special he is before you see any development in his own expectations.

In the early days of our company I met a guy who had seen some tough times. He had had no real success in his adult life at all. But there was something I liked right away. I could just tell that underneath all the pain and discouragement, there was talent and a lot of feeling. I spent a lot of time with him, and I worked at building his own expectations.

Today, his portrait hangs on our company's "Wall of Fame." He's experienced great success, and has achieved things that he never thought possible when he joined our company. I didn't perform any miracles; the talent and desire were already there. All I did was help him feel better about himself, help him realize that he could make it. The best part is that, along the way, we built a special kind of love for each other.

Push-Up Principle

Your encouragement helps your people compete.

In athletics, one of the most important things you have to teach players is how to compete. When you encourage your people and build their expectations, you're helping them prepare for competition in the business world. Sometimes they'll be outnumbered by opponents, sometimes it will seem like everything's going wrong and everyone's against them. In that kind of situation, often the only thing that will keep them hanging on is their inner strength.

Every time you encourage people or let them know that you believe they can succeed, you build a little bit more of that inner strength. You build that little reserve that can be the difference between whether your people throw in the towel or stick it out until they win.

You've got to let them know, every day in every way, that you expect to come out of the game a winner, and you expect that from them, too. Just keep "pushing them up" and you'll be surprised at how fast they start learning to rise on their own.

Chapter 12

Get Your Priorities Straight

Management Mistake

Many managers place their career above everything else.

Leadership Solution

Successful leaders know the importance of living a balanced life.

The race to succeed, and to help other people become successful isn't a sprint, it's a marathon. There's a lot to remember and a lot to do along the course, and it all takes time and energy. Sometimes it seems like there aren't enough hours in a day to do what you should. It can seem like a juggling act to balance all the demands of your time.

I believe that the only way you can begin to effectively be successful in business is to set priorities in all areas of your life. Only by making a conscious decision about what's most important to you, and structuring your life to include those things, can you begin to reduce your anxiety and achieve a balance in your life.

One of the saddest things I see in business today is the belief that, to be successful, you must devote 100 percent of your time to your work. The idea of the busy executive who never sees his family because he spends all his time at the office is almost accepted as normal. As a result, people who enter the business world with a burning desire to succeed assume that they've got to put their job before everything else in order to get to the top. They develop a single-mindedness about work that causes them to neglect other important areas of their lives.

Push-Up Principle

Setting priorities helps to establish balance and perspective.

If you want to be a success, you've got to work harder than the other guy. You've got to pay the price. You've got to do what it takes and a little bit more. I've talked a lot in this book about making the extra effort required to achieve great things. But don't think for a minute that I believe that your business comes before everything else in your life.

In my life, the priorities are God first, family second, and business third. Within those areas, I try to structure my life in a way that strikes a balance between the physical, the emotional and the spiritual and allow time to develop each area.

Push-Up Principle

Faith and hope come from a strong spiritual commitment.

You know, in our modern world, a lot of people don't want to think about their spiritual life. When things are going well in their careers, they get to feeling that they don't need anything else. Sometimes, they get out there in business and they even start to think that all those lessons they learned back in Sunday school when they were young don't apply any more. The "do unto others" principle is OK for church, but you can't really follow it in business, right? You've got to do whatever's necessary, whether it's right or wrong.

I believe that kind of thinking can be one of the biggest mistakes you'll ever make in your business life. Now, I'm not here to tell you how to worship God or what church you should attend. That's a personal decision. But, I am telling you that if you don't have your spiritual life in order, if you don't think the Judeo-Christian principles of right and wrong, and good or bad, apply to you, then you're in for a rude awakening somewhere down the road. If you don't lead a decent moral life — and encourage your people to do the same — I believe you just won't enjoy long-term success and happiness.

I know from my experience working with thousands of people that the ones who hang on when times are tough, and are able to face adversity without giving up, are the people who have a strong spiritual life. Besides many other things, trying to live a godly life builds two ingredients that are essential to success —faith and hope. I've found that it's the people who have strong religious convictions that see setbacks and disappointments as no more than stumbling blocks along the road. They can face the toughest times knowing that they're not alone, that they have support to lean on. And they have faith that things will work out for the best no matter how dark it looks that moment.

Push-Up Principle

It is possible to balance a busy work life with a rich, rewarding family life.

The second area to consider in living a balanced life is your family life. I just can't emphasize this area enough, because it's the area that more people take for granted than any other. As I visit with people all across the country, I see firsthand the heartaches that can be caused when family life takes a back seat to business. It wasn't meant to be that way, and it won't work. No matter how much you want to be successful, you can't expect to just put your family "on hold" until you become a millionaire. If you do, chances are good that, when you finally get to the top, you'll be there all alone.

Because sales is a demanding business, people constantly ask questions about how to balance their business and family lives.

The answer isn't that complicated. You've simply got to take some of the same principles we've talked about using to succeed in business, and apply those principles to your family life as well. You've got to treat your family good, just like you treat your people in business; you've got to invest the time and energy to make your marriage work just like you invest it to make your business work; you've got to have high goals for building a rewarding marriage and family life, and work toward those goals.

One of our company's national sales directors had a great response when he was asked how he managed the difficult balancing act between family and work. "I don't have any fancy methods," he said. "If you really put your spouse and children before your work, you find ways to spend time with them; you may not have as much time as you'd like, but you make it quality time. If you've got your priorities right, you just handle it."

This guy doesn't buy the philosophy that there aren't enough hours in the day for both. When he does have time off from work, he doesn't spend it out playing golf with the guys or going off on a hunting trip alone. He spends his spare time with his family doing something they all enjoy. His wife helps out in his business, and they share dreams for the future. He doesn't make work something that his wife has no part of, and they enjoy the benefits of shared effort toward the same goal.

A newcomer to our business, who had just begun to move ahead after a few years of struggling, shared the secret to his turnaround in business. "My business life changed for the better when I fell in love with my wife again," he said. He, like so many people, had shortchanged his family for the sake of his business, and had forgotten about the difference that family love and support can make.

Don't deny your family the time they need from you, and don't deny yourself the support and pleasure of your family. Most important, don't forget that they're one of the major reasons you're working so hard in the first place!

Push-Up Principles

Good health is necessary in order to work effectively, and to enjoy the fruits of your efforts.

It's important to remember that your physical life counts, too. General George Patton once said, "An active mind cannot exist in an inactive body." Personal health is one of the most often ignored areas of life; yet it's the one area that, if abused, can literally destroy the pleasure of all the others.

It's so sad when people spend years working toward a goal, only to find when they reach it that they don't have the good health to enjoy the rewards of all their efforts.

A healthy diet is the single most important aspect of maintaining a healthy body. Over the years we've been conditioned to eat a refined, high-fat, high-cholesterol, high-salt diet. We eat fast-foods, whatever's convenient, and our taste buds begin to crave the things that are harmful to us physically.

There's abundant information today pointing to the error of our ways and educating us to a diet of mainly vegetables, fruits, and natural grains. Medical science is gradually moving toward an interest in prevention and wellness. It takes a great amount of discipline to change this area of your life, but it's so important to be well and healthy.

Exercise is the number two priority. I know it's difficult to find time. When a long day is stretching out in front of me, and I've got a million things I need to do, it's tempting to skip my morning jog. But I make an effort to keep it up, because I know the small amount of time it takes will pay off in dividends like more energy and a better feeling about myself. Plus, sometimes I do my best thinking while jogging around my home or down the street near one of the many hotels where I stay on the road.

Neglect in this area will come back to haunt you later in life. If you get back to basics and ask yourself, "What is really important in my life?" you're sure to conclude that health is right up there near the top of the list. You simply can't afford not to make time for your physical development.

Push-Up Principle
A leader must be an example of balanced living.

Just as in all the other areas we've talked about, you can set an example of balanced living in your own life. Let your people see that you have thought about your priorities, and are striving for a balance between the spiritual life, family life, and business life. Let your people know that you don't expect them to abandon their families or their religious lives in order to succeed in your business.

As a leader, you want your people to have an exceptional interest in their work. But, you don't want them to see everything in their lives in terms of their work. I've heard a lot of sales leaders encourage people to join clubs, like the Rotary Club or the Jaycees, in order to increase their sales prospects. I don't believe in that sort of thing. If you want to join a club or community organization, fine, but I believe that you should join those organizations for the right reasons — to help your community or to build new friendships in your neighborhood. You shouldn't use organizations, and the people in them, solely as a way to increase your own business. I believe that if you're a good salesman, and you believe in what you're doing for people, you will just naturally find sales "prospects" anywhere you are. Don't join things solely for that purpose. Your intentions will be false, and it will seem that way to the other people in the club. And, if you encourage that kind of false participation, your people may see you as a calculating, insincere person.

Get your life in control, have a harmony and balance that allows for personal growth, family growth, and spiritual growth. You'll feel better about yourself, and your people will see that they can achieve that kind of balance in their own lives.

Chapter 13

Know Where You're Going

Management Mistake

People can't lead others if they have no clear direction themselves.

Leadership Solution

Leaders set goals in all areas of their lives.

So many people never get anywhere in their lives because they don't know where they are trying to go. If you don't have a destination in your career, and in your life, how are you going to make any plans? If you don't know where *you're* going, how are you ever going to help anyone else reach their destination?

Push-Up Principle

The most successful people are those who set goals early in life.

A few years ago I heard about a study that was done at Harvard University. The graduating class was polled, and it was found that only 3 percent of the class had any clear goals set for their future. Twenty years later, the researchers followed up on that same graduating class. Guess who had turned out to be the most successful? The 3 percent who had clearly defined goals accomplished more and made more money than the other 97 percent combined.

There's nothing mysterious about it. It makes sense that if you don't know what you want to do with your life, or what you want to accomplish, you won't ever establish a working plan of action.

To really move ahead, you need short-term goals and long-term goals. You need to know where you want to be six months from now and two years from now...even 10 years from now.

Now, don't get me wrong. There's nothing wrong with making changes in your goals as you go along. It's important to be flexible. But the most important thing is to make a conscious choice about what you want to achieve and how you're going to get there.

It took me a long time to learn this lesson myself. I wanted to be a football coach. I worked hard at it, and I had winning teams. Things were going well, but unfortunately, I just wasn't doing well enough financially to support my family. In my heart, I had the goal of becoming financially independent, being able to earn enough so that we wouldn't always be dreading the monthly bills. I wanted to be able to pursue my own business interests, and not be dependent on anyone else to decide how far I could go.

That's a lot to want, and there I was, a small-town football coach in south Georgia, making next to nothing, and working part-time jobs on the side to make ends meet.

Finally I got so frustrated, so tired of always scraping by and not having the freedom that I wanted, that I stopped waiting around for somebody to come along and give me a million dollars and my own business. I had to face the hard truth that, if I wanted a million dollars, I was going to have to come up with a plan, make it work, and go get the business and the million dollars myself.

That's when things started to turn around for me. I had to make some hard decisions. The hardest was deciding that I would never achieve my goals by coaching football, although that was something I loved doing. But if I had never taken that hard look at my life, I might never have taken the steps that finally led to reaching the goals I had for me and my family.

Now, you don't want to be like me and struggle for years and years before you realize that basic fact. Wherever you are in your career, stop right now and analyze what you want, what your goals are, and begin a specific plan to reach them. Know what you want, and work toward it every day.

Push-Up Principle

Have specific goals, and a specific plan for reaching them.

Almost anyone who's been around me for long has heard me sing the praises of *Think and Grow Rich,* a great book by Napoleon Hill. The book is the outcome of a lifetime of studying successful people to discover the qualities they all share. Based on these "common denominators," Hill came up with a basic formula for success. After reading the book, I applied these formulas to my life and saw an immediate change in my mental attitude and real results in my business life.

Hill discovered that setting specific goals and working out a specific plan to achieve them was one of the "common denominators" among winners. He outlined a six-step plan that went something like this:

1) Have a specific goal; 2) Set a specific time in which to achieve your goal; 3) Develop a plan to achieve your goal; 4) Decide what kind of price you are willing to pay; 5) Write it down; and 6) Think about reaching your goal every day.

Six simple steps — but there is a power in those steps that has been proven time and time again by great leaders in business. When I finally got serious about achieving my goals, I applied Hill's formula. At the time, in 1969, I was earning $10,700 a year as an athletic director and football coach. I decided that my specific goal would be to establish a guaranteed income of $30,000 a year for life. Knowing that I had that amount set aside would give me the security I was after. I wrote my goal down on a little piece of cardboard that I could put on my calendar.

My next step was to decide that I would be totally financially independent in 10 years at age 38. I had saved $40,000 in the two and one-half years I had spent working part-time in addition to coaching. I figured that I could save my $40,000 at 10% for 10 years, and turn it into $100,000, plus interest. Figuring I needed $300,000 cash, which at 10% would allow me to withdraw $30,000 each year without touching the principal, I was still $200,000 short. Again using 10% interest, I would have to save $1,000 a month for 10 years to get the extra $200,000. Finally, I had it — my plan for reaching my goal of $30,000 a year for life!

I knew saving $1,000 each month would be tough, but that was what it was going to take. I decided on my "price." I would give up coaching to build financial security for me and my family. Last, I kept my goal in my mind, and I thought about it every single day, especially at times when I felt like I wanted to quit. Hill's formula worked for me, and it will work for anybody, simply because it forces you to think about what you want, plan how you will achieve it, and decide what price you'll pay for your dreams to come true. After you've done that, the rest of it is just plain old hard work. But if you don't take those beginning steps to sort things out in your mind, you may work hard all your career and still not reach your goals.

Push-Up Principle
Discover "The Magic Of 90 Days."

It's important to remember that there are two types of goals, short-term goals and long-term goals. The long-term goals are the big goals, and they come first — like my goal of $30,000 a year for life. After you've decided on those, it's important to establish a series of short-term goals that will provide you with day-to-day motivation. I've found that it's useful for me to set a time frame that gives me enough time to take some serious action, but isn't so far off into the future that I am tempted to postpone my activity.

That's the best thing about short-term goals. They establish a sense of urgency; they provide you with a deadline in the near future that prompts action.

I believe in "The Magic Of 90 Days." Anyone can do anything for 90 days. In our company, for example, you might set a goal of making 10 sales a week. Then, you'd make the decision to do whatever it takes to make those 10 sales a week for 90 days and work like a maniac. What you couldn't keep up for two years, you can force yourself to keep up for 90 days.

The positive results are amazing! At the end of that period, you've got a great feeling about yourself, you've accomplished something that will pay off financially, and you're ready to celebrate. The special benefit is that, once you've proven to yourself that you can make 10 sales a week, your regular goal of five or six sales will seem like a breeze.

I know that the 90-day commitment is magic, because I've seen it work time and time again. At a retreat in Tennessee, two sales leaders listened to a speech on the subject and talked about it on their car trip back home. Both decided to give it a try. They gave it a tremendous effort. The first 30 days, not much happened. The second 30 days were better. Then, the last 30 days, their businesses exploded, thanks to all their effort in the previous two months. Both experienced fantastic improvements in their incomes —and in their self-confidence. One even did so well that he was promoted at the end of his 90-day period!

The magic of 90 days can work for anyone, if they really commit to the effort. I've seen 30-day and 60-day commitments work well, too. It's just human nature that you need a series of little victories on the way to achieving your big goals. The short term commitment provides motivation and encouragement to keep pushing ahead.

Push-Up Principle

Reward yourself when you achieve goals; punish yourself when you don't.

We've talked about the importance of setting both long and short-term goals. But there's one more important element to goal-setting. In order for your goal-setting to be effective, you need some system of reinforcement, some way of rewarding yourself when you stick to your schedule and reach one of your short-term goals. The other side of that is that you also need a way to "punish" yourself if you don't accomplish what you set out to do. I don't know why, but positive and negative reinforcement really works. It sets up an expectation in your mind of some real result that will occur at the end of your efforts.

My second head coaching job was a brand new high school in Columbus, Georgia. Only the first three high school levels were to be taught there the first year, so I didn't even have a senior class to draw from for my team. My job was to build a football program from the ground up. We were starting with nothing; no uniforms, no helmets, nothing. The sportswriters had listed us last in the region in their season predictions.

The first day that I met with my new team, we set a goal of becoming state champions. I put a big banner up on the bulletin board, so that would be the first thing the players saw every day when they came to practice. We made a commitment to being number one.

Once we had set our big goal (and it was a pretty big one, considering our situation), we set a smaller goal of getting better with every game we played. After each game, we would try to measure how much we had improved.

We measured our success both in terms of offensive effort and defensive effort. For example, if we won by more than 21 points, that was an offensive victory. If we won by holding the team scoreless, then it was a defensive victory.

After each game, the players knew what to expect. You see, Monday was a tough practice day when the team worked out with heavy pads and all their equipment. If they won, they came to practice on Monday in shorts. We'd have a light practice, just loosen up a little bit, and go home.

If the team won, but didn't show any improvement from the week before, we'd put on our heavy pads and have an extra long, extra hard practice. Maybe we'd do 40 wind sprints instead of our usual 10.

But, if the team lost, we'd practice on Saturday. Then, we'd go all out and practice like maniacs. Believe me, nobody wanted to even think about those Saturday practices.

That's what you've got to do in your own life, and with your people. If you're doing great in your business efforts, reward yourself. Take an afternoon off and go on a picnic with your family, or take a weekend trip.

But if you're getting beaten by the competition, have a "Saturday practice." Pull out all the stops and work twice as long and twice as hard as you planned to work. The point is that if you're doing badly, you've got to do something different to break your losing streak.

Even if you're doing pretty well, but you're not improving, you've got to change your method. You should never be satisfied with winning but not improving. When that happens, you need to try something different to get some momentum going that will turn the situation around.

Reward and punishment are powerful tools for group goal-setting, too. In our company, many leaders hold little "contests" that promise a reward if group goals are met and punishment if they're not. It can be something simple, like a steak dinner for the winners and beans for the losers, but it gets the point across. It's a fabulous motivational tool; it can be a lot of fun, and it gets real results.

It has worked well for me in business dozens of times. It worked for the football team in Columbus, too. That brand new team won like crazy. We were the talk of the town. We didn't win the state, but we almost made it. We were the only team in Georgia to ever win the regional championship in its first year of conference play. Fifteen years later, our record still stands.

Push-Up Principle

The day you start setting goals, you're a day closer to success.

I can't leave this section without mentioning one of the biggest dangers to achieving your goals —procrastination. We all do it, so nobody thinks too much about it. But continually putting off goal-setting is far more likely to result in failure than any event or incident that will happen to you once you're on your way.

The very best advice I can offer on setting goals and making plans is: *Do it today.* Don't wait until tomorrow or next week. Don't think you're too busy or too tired right now. The longer you put it off, the more settled you'll get in your present situation, and the easier it will seem to just drift along where you are right now.

Take the time today, this weekend at the latest, to get off to yourself and think about your goals and desires. Talk to your spouse about your goals, and involve him or her in the decision-making process. No matter how old you are, it's not too late to set goals and achieve them. Get serious about your future. When you start seeing your goals turn into realities, you'll wish that you had started planning and goal-setting years earlier!

Push-Up Principle

The first step to a goal is a dream.

To win, you've got to have ability and the right attitude. You've got to have toughness and determination. But before anything else, you've got to have a dream. Your dream is the glue that holds all the effort together. It's the one thing that, once you have it, no one can ever take away from you.

One of the saddest things I see around me today is that most people have stopped dreaming. Our world today is so competitive and so tough that young people starting out sometimes get a lot of hard knocks. Before they've had a chance to develop their potential, they get beaten down by how tough it is. The enthusiasm they once had turns to bitterness, and they decide to just "settle" for whatever hand they are dealt. The older people get, the more and more they forget how to dream; they think that dreaming is only for children, not adults.

I believe that to win in life, you've got to become a dreamer again. You've got to become excited and "turned on" about your life and your future. The greatest thing about this country is that you can become what you dream about. I know it's tough, but it's possible. And all most people really need is to know that there's a chance — an opportunity — for their dreams to come true. If you want something badly enough, you can still achieve it, even in a complicated world like ours.

I believe that when you approach people to join your company, you can't just sell them a job. People are sick of jobs; they've had other jobs, and, many times, they've not been good experiences. I think we've forgotten that people aren't really looking for guarantees. All they want is a chance. They don't want you to just offer them a job, they want you to offer them a dream and the opportunity to make it come true. If you can offer people a chance to do something special with their lives, a chance to believe in something, a chance to dream again, you've given them the kind of motivation to succeed that they'll never have if you just give them a set of duties.

And never underestimate the power of dreaming. I believe that having a dream to strive for just may be the one quality that gives you that "edge" over most ordinary people. We've all heard the expression that someone "has his heart set" on something. I've always liked that expression. All your success, and the success of your people is, in the end, built on desire. No matter what the odds are against you, if you've "set your heart" on something, you'll have the determination and the motivation to see it through to the end.

Become a dreamer again. Encourage the dreams of your people. Once you've got a dream, you can set goals, build your plans, and act. But until you start dreaming, what you do in your life may just be action without purpose, and that won't lead to real fulfillment. Woodrow Wilson, our twenty-eighth president, said, "We grow great by dreams. All big men are dreamers...some of us let dreams die, but others nourish and protect them, nurse them through bad days...to the sunshine and light which always comes...."

Push-Up Principle

Goals are not just for business, but for all areas of your life.

One last word on goals — I believe that you set goals in all areas of your life, not just in your business career. Your life consists of more than your work. You have certain desires for your family; you have personal desires, you have spiritual and emotional desires. These other areas are just as important as your career or your business.

You can use the procedures I've outlined for setting goals in all areas of your life. Sitting down with your family and deciding on family goals can be one of the most rewarding experiences you'll ever have. Determining your own personal goals and working toward them can cause great improvements in your own personality and self-image. Setting goals for your spiritual improvement can work miracles in your life.

Once you get into a habit of goal-setting, you'll wonder how you ever managed to accomplish anything before. As far as your people are concerned, helping them establish their goals will be one of the most helpful things that you can do for them as a leader.

Chapter 14

Don't Be Afraid To Fail

Management Mistake

Many managers let their fear of failure keep them from achieving real success.

Leadership Solution

You must take chances in order to have great success.

If someone asked you who had more strikeouts during his time than anyone else, who would you say? Chances are your answer wouldn't be Babe Ruth, the home run king. But it's true.

Besides hitting more home runs than anyone else, he also struck out more times than anyone else.

There's a big message for all of us in that statistic. If you're going to succeed, it means that you're going to make mistakes along the way. If you're going to dare mighty things, you're very likely to fall flat a few times in the process. Winning big means taking a lot of chances.

So what? Isn't winning worth the risks? If you reach your goals, you'll be remembered, not for your mistakes, but for what you accomplished. Nobody remembers Babe Ruth's strikeouts. They only remember that he was one of the all-time great hitters in the history of baseball.

Still, it's amazing how many people never go after the things they want in life because they are scared to death of failing. That fear holds people back ten times more often than lack of talent, lack of intelligence, or lack of opportunity. In order to really succeed, and lead others to success, you've got to overcome that big obstacle, your fear of failing.

Push-Up Principle

Don't waste time and energy worrying about things that haven't happened.

In my early years at our company, I had a great manager who taught me something I'll never forget. "Art," he said, "remember this. Ninety-nine percent of the things you fear never happen. So stop worrying. Just go out there and follow your instincts." That advice has stood me in good stead throughout my business life.

The best way to stop worrying is to learn to trust your own instincts. It's a requirement because, in a lot of situations, you can't just follow a manual or call back to the home office when there's a problem. You've got to develop a feel for what action to take at a particular time. You've got to have your finger on the pulse of your people and the business. When you're in the middle of a situation that requires immediate action, you can't think about it forever. You've got to be able to trust your own instincts and make a decision, without fearing the consequences.

Playwright George Bernard Shaw once said, "Common sense is instinct. Enough of it is genius." You'd think you'd never have to tell anyone to use their common sense. It seems so obvious. But many people put all their faith in "book sense," instead of trusting the knowledge that comes from their own experience and just plain everyday living.

Partly it's a matter of confidence. New managers sometimes have trouble seeing themselves as decision-makers, especially if their decision-making skills haven't been tested. They're inclined to rely on the ideas and opinions of others, instead of their own "gut feeling" about a situation. They look back later and realize that their own instincts were right all along.

Sometimes it's wise to seek the counsel of others. But I'd encourage anyone to worry a little bit less about what someone else would do and rely a little bit more on the simple common sense God gave them.

Push-Up Principle

When people are running scared, they make more mistakes than ever.

One thing that I learned as a coach is that the more a player is worried about making mistakes, the more mistakes he makes. You've probably experienced the same thing in your own life. When you feel that you have to do something perfectly, you suddenly fall apart.

You can't let fear have that kind of hold on you. You can prepare to win, do everything you can to improve your chances of winning, and then you've just got to go out there and let it all hang out and play. If things don't work out, well, you did all you could, and you'll just have to try harder to prepare better the next time.

As a coach, I'd have a meeting with my team every fall before the season started, and I'd give them this talk that was half-humorous, half-serious. I'd say, "Fellows, you're the luckiest people that ever played football. While you were out there messing around this summer, I was working my butt off getting ready for football season. I analyzed our films, I went to coaching clinics, I read books. And I've put together a playbook that you won't believe. It's got the best plays in football. There are no bad plays in this playbook. When you're out there in practice, just tell yourself, 'Boy, I'm the luckiest kid in football 'cause Coach Williams has analyzed this thing, and we have a playbook with no bad plays.' Another thing you've got going for you this year is that you have the best play caller in all of football. He never calls a bad play. And that play caller is me.

"How can we lose? We don't have any bad plays and we have the best play caller in football who never calls a bad play.

"So when you're out there in the huddle on Friday night, and I send you in a play, you just say to yourself, 'Boy, I'm the luckiest kid that ever played football because Coach Williams is the best play caller in the world and he doesn't call any bad plays.' "

What I was saying to my players was true. I was a good play caller, and every play in our playbook was designed to work. But you know what happened in reality? Most plays gained a yard or two or lost a yard or two, or we missed a block, or dropped a pass or fumbled the ball. Ninety-five percent of the time the plays didn't turn out like they were supposed to.

That's the way it turns out with the plays you call as a business leader, too. They may be great plays, but in practice, they don't turn out like they are supposed to.

But the teams that win are the teams that believe those plays are the best plays. The winning teams have the courage to keep calling those plays even though they don't work 95 percent of the time. They know the plays will fail — a lot — but they keep practicing them and trying them out in the field, and all of a sudden, the plays work and they win. That's the way it works in business, too! When you know you're doing what's right, just keep on trying, keep on practicing, and all of a sudden it will work.

So many people are so scared of failing that they won't even try. When they meet their first defeat, they lose all their courage and all their confidence. If you're going to win, you've got to keep fighting and competing.

Push-Up Principle
Eliminate the four basic "failure fears" from your business life.

In business, I see four basic fears: 1) fear of competition, 2) fear of controversy, 3) fear of what other people say, and 4) fear of things you can't control.

Fear of competition is one of the major fears among business people. In the free enterprise system, you're always going to have competition. The competition is always going to talk, they're always going to be coming out with new products and new ideas, and they're always going to be saying they'll put you out of business. You can't get sidetracked worrying about the competition. You beat them by concentrating on your own business, not worrying about theirs.

Fear of controversy is one of the toughest fears you have to deal with in American business. If you go out there and become a crusader, and try to do something different, people are going to shoot at you like you won't believe. They'll attack you, they'll say bad things about you, they'll try to pull you back down and keep you from succeeding. That's just the way it is.

The best way to overcome fear of controversy is to sit back and look at the alternative. If you can't take the controversy and criticism, you can always go back to being average and ordinary. Then everybody will like you, everybody will be your buddy. All the average, ordinary, frustrated, unhappy people who don't have the courage or commitment to "go for it" will join up with you and talk about the people who are successful.

Remember, you're only here on this earth for a flicker, just a whisper out of time. If you're happy being among the 98 percent who are average and ordinary, that's fine. But if you've set a goal to be somebody special, to do something special with your life, you may have to make a choice between that and popularity. Fear of what other people say is very similar to fear of controversy, but I'm thinking here about people close to you, like your friends and family.

I can easily use myself as an example of this kind of fear. When I was introduced to the insurance concept that finally led me to form A.L. Williams, I really got excited. Here was something I could really believe in. Here was something I really wanted to spread the word about. There was just one problem. I didn't want to be an insurance salesman.

Let's face it. Insurance salesmen are not the most popular people in most people's minds.

I did start selling, but every time one of my relatives, or one of my wife's relatives, asked me what I was doing, I just couldn't seem to get out the words, "selling insurance." I kept making fancy names for myself to hide what I really did.

It took being able to see the good that I was doing for clients, and experiencing financial success before I was really able to be proud of myself and my profession. I should have been proud all along, because I knew what I was doing was right and I believed in it. But that just goes to show how mixed up you can get when you put your opinion of your worth in the hands of other people. If I had given up on my crusade because of what others said, not only would I have hurt myself, but the thousands of people our business eventually helped would have been hurt, too.

Keep your goals in front of you, believe in yourself and your personal cause, and don't worry about what others think. It's what you think about what you do that's important.

Fear of things you can't control is something we're all guilty of to some degree, both in and out of business. Just watch the national news one night and you can hear enough to keep you busy worrying for a year. Every day you hear of so many bad things, negative things, it's easy to think the world is going to end soon and nothing is worth doing. Every day people do things or events happen that you can't control.

A friend of mine has an annual cookout for his people. Every year his wife worries for weeks that it will rain on the day of the cookout. Over and over, my friend tells her not to worry, but she still does. And, you know what, it has *never* rained on the day of the cookout so far! Since there isn't a single thing she could do to prevent the rain anyway, the time she spends worrying is wasted time.

I've found out that all you can control is you, your attitude and your activity. I've developed the philosophy that life is too short to worry about things I can't control. I'm going to make my contribution, the best I can. When my time is over, I want to be able to look back and say, "You know, Art, you were a decent guy. You really made a contribution, you're somebody to be proud of."

I'm going to accomplish what I want to accomplish. The bad things in the world affect my life, but they can't affect my personal goals and commitments. You've got your life to live, and you've got to live it the best you can in today's world and save your energy for accomplishing something that will have positive results.

Push-Up Principle
You can't hold anything back if you want to win.

There's another kind of fear that people have that is harder to spot, especially in themselves. That's the fear of giving it everything you've got. Some people hold just a little bit in reserve, because as long as they don't make their best effort, they are able to justify their failure. They can always say, "Well, I could have succeeded if I had really given it all I had." I'm well acquainted with that fear, because it was one of my biggest problems.

Several years ago, I was a successful salesman for another company. I was doing well, and my family was secure. Yet I really wasn't doing what I wanted to do. In my mind, I wanted to launch out, to make a real move toward total success. But I was so scared I would fail that I couldn't give it all I had.

So, I always held a little something back. I'd just think to myself, "Well, I'll really do it next time."

But you know, one day several years ago, I looked in the mirror and I didn't like who I saw. I didn't like myself. I failed the "mirror test." I saw a man who didn't live up to his potential. I saw somebody afraid to really take a chance. At that moment, I determined for once I was going all out. I was going to give it all I had, and if I failed, at least I would know I had given it my best shot.

The strangest thing happened when I made that decision. For the first time, everything fell into place. Once I decided that I was totally committed to what I was doing, I really started to succeed. Oh, there were a million problems. But my attitude was so totally different that nothing fazed me; I felt as if I could cope with anything.

When you make that kind of commitment, you know that "this is it." You know you can't back down. And until you do, that possibility of quitting is always hiding in the back of your mind. Once you know this is your best shot, you just can't entertain the idea of quitting. And that makes all the difference in your performance.

Push-Up Principle
All you can do is all you can do.

Sometimes, no matter what you do, no matter how much you try, things don't turn out the way you've planned. You may work around the clock, you may pay a tremendous price, you may be totally committed, and still find that the direction you've taken just isn't going to work out. Sometimes, there are situations that occur that you just can't control, in spite of your best efforts. This is the time when a lot of people despair and want to quit. They feel like they've failed because they just couldn't turn events around.

This is never a pleasant situation, even when it happens on a small scale. But this is the kind of situation that happens to almost everyone at some point in their lives.

A favorite saying of mine is, "All you can do is all you can do." When you've done all you can with a situation, you've followed every avenue you know to resolving it, there's only one thing left to do. You need to accept the situation, accept the fact that you've taken a wrong turn or come face-to-face with a situation that you can't control. And then, you've got to start moving forward again. It may mean changing directions or working toward your goals from another angle. But what you can't do is worry yourself crazy about it, or let it defeat you and destroy your commitment to succeed.

There's also a second part to my saying, "All you can do is all you can do — *but all you can do is enough.*" When you've truly made your best effort, you've done enough. You've done everything anyone could do, and that's all that anyone expects of you, and all you can expect of yourself. Don't ever be defeated by a misstep in your career. Just try to keep in mind another of my favorite sayings, "Success is never certain, and failure is never final."

Work every day on eliminating fear from your life, and helping your people do the same. You'll know when you've succeeded at eliminating fear, because you'll be miles out in front of everyone else, and your people will be right there with you.

Chapter 15

You've Got To Pay The Price

Management Mistake

Many people want a fast, easy road to riches and success.

Leadership Solution

Every big achievement has a big price.

Everyone wants to be financially independent; everybody wants to be hugely successful. But everybody doesn't reach those goals; in fact, a lot of people don't. Why? I believe that it's because only a small percentage of the people who work are willing to "pay the price" that's required for great success.

I don't know how many times I've heard some business person say, "It's not how hard you work, but how smart you work, that makes the difference." I don't believe that for a minute.

There's never been an Olympic champion that hasn't worked a killing schedule for years and years and years to be the best. I don't know of any super-successful businessman who hasn't paid a fantastic price to get to the top.

Thomas Edison, our nation's most famous inventor, said, "Genius is 1% inspiration and 99% perspiration. I never did anything worth doing by accident, nor did any of my inventions come by accident. They came by hard work."

It would be wonderful to be able to tell you in this book some "secret" for getting to the top and being a winner without paying the price for success. But I can't, because there just is no easy way.

Push-Up Principle
The harder you work, the luckier you get.

Whenever someone suddenly comes into the public eye because of some big accomplishments, there's the tendency for other people to say, "he was just lucky." Usually, if you look a little deeper, these "lucky" people have worked years and years to get to their level of achievement and success.

There's just no substitute for hard work. If there is a "secret" to success, this is probably it. The person who works the longest and the hardest, and with the most intensity, is the person who's going the farthest.

I believe you can beat 50 percent of the people out there by just working hard. Most people won't work hard enough or long enough to win, so you've got half the folks licked if you can just keep working. You beat another 40 percent by living right, finding something you believe in and having decent morals and principles.

So, if you just work hard and live right, you can be in the top 10 percent. In the free enterprise system, the top 10 percent is a dogfight, plain and simple, and you've got to fight it out the rest of the way. In my experience, the people who win big are the people who are willing to pay the price for success. Nothing good comes easy. In the free enterprise system, you've got to work for it. Vince Lombardi, one of the most famous football coaches of all time, said, "The dictionary is the only place that *success* comes before *work*. Hard work is the price we must pay for success. I think you can accomplish almost anything if you're willing to pay the price."

I used to tell my football team before our Friday night game, "Fellows, listen, you'd better come ready to play tomorrow. You're going to have to show up and fight. Those folks in the wrong-colored jerseys aren't going to roll over and play dead. If you want to win the game, you've got to come ready to play. When you put that uniform on, you'd better strap it on tight, and you'd better go out and compete."

I see adults who roll out of bed every morning and put their uniforms on. They show up to work and they just take it and take it and take it. They never fight, they never learn to compete. They expect defeat, right from the beginning, and defeat is what they get. Life gives them just what they are willing to fight for and compete for.

Push-Up Principle
Sacrifice is a part of paying the price.

If you're going to make your dreams come true, you're going to have to sacrifice. Now, sacrifice is a word people don't want to hear. It's one of what I call the "tough words." But it's the only one I know to use, because that's just the way it is.

— Sacrifice means giving up a few selfish hobbies to further your dreams. I don't know anybody who wins big who has hobbies.

— Sacrifice means turning off the TV to spend quality time with your family or study and work to improve yourself.

— Sacrifice means denying yourself something you want until you have achieved your goals. Sometimes, it means doing without something you *need* if it puts you a step closer to your goals.

A woman in our company stands out in my mind as an example of sacrifice. She wanted success so badly, and she was willing to pay a tremendous price for it. By the time she found our company, she and her husband had already paid a big price. They lost everything they had in a bad farming year. The family moved, looking for more opportunity. Both took jobs, and they got up early and stayed late trying to catch up from their loss. Still, they could barely make ends meet. The whole family was under pressure, and the strain was becoming unbearable.

Yet, when she came to our company, she came all the way. Somewhere she got the courage to make an intense effort one more time. There were serious doubts that she could ever make it, but she never doubted herself, in spite of past events, and her husband and family never doubted her. From the first, she worked a grueling schedule. It took time to build her business, and her husband and children made many sacrifices to allow her the time to get started.

Today, she's a senior vice president and one of the top leaders in the company. She has a personal crusade to help other people in positions of hardship get a fresh start in her business. More than anyone I know, she understood the price of success, and was willing to pay that price to escape from a situation of dependence and deprivation.

If you're going to really win, sacrifice can't be just a sometime thing. When things are good, you don't stop paying the price. You don't lean back and take time off as soon as you've achieved a little bit of success.

I've seen this happen so many times in business. People start making some money, maybe more than they have ever made before, and they forget about their goal of financial independence. They go out soon and buy the big house and the new car and take the dream vacation. Then, the first time things go back the other way, and they usually do, they're in trouble again.

If your goal is financial independence, live below your means until you reach your goal. Don't start spending money until you've achieved your dream. Then you'll be ready to enjoy all the good things.

Sacrifice also means that you don't stop paying the price when things go bad. When everything seems to be falling apart, there's always a temptation to say, "Oh, forget it. I can't bounce back from this one. Who cares? I knew I couldn't make it." But you can, if you'll just hang on. As I said before, things are never as good or as bad as they seem. If you can stick it out, and work hard, things will turn around. The hardest thing in the world is to keep on paying the price and keep dreaming when things are going bad, but it's the only way if you're going to win.

Self-discipline is the "inner" quality that's necessary before you can keep working and paying the price until you win. No one else can make you put in those extra hours or that extra effort. It has to come from inside, and it requires that you develop the toughness to turn down an immediate pleasure today for success and financial security in the future. The sacrifices you make now will seem so small when you've made it that you'll wonder why you were ever tempted.

Push-Up Principle
The greater the rewards — the greater the price.

There's a lot of people who think that not everybody has to pay the price. That's dead wrong. Everybody has to pay a price of one kind or another.

There are a lot of people out there who refuse to compete, refuse to work hard, refuse to look at life as a challenge and pay a price. But I think that those people do pay a price by not competing, not sacrificing, and not trying to become the best person they can become. I believe that their price is not feeling good about themselves, not having any dreams or any ambitions, not having financial security, and not being able to do the things they want to do for themselves and their families. The saddest kind of life, and the biggest kind of price, in my opinion, goes to these people.

The other kind of people go out there and they fight and they work hard and sacrifice, and they win. They have an opportunity to become somebody they're proud of. They enjoy all the great things that life has to offer. They feel good about themselves.

Push-Up Principle
Winning is better than you ever imagined.

The thing that stands in the way of most people being able to pay a big price is that they don't have any idea of how good it is to win.

You know, when I was really struggling in my early years in sales and management, I dreamed about what it would be like to be financially independent. I dreamed all the time about being my own boss and having the freedom to have my own business and work toward my own goals. I thought it would be wonderful to have all those things. But I had to pay the price to have those things. And while I was paying the price, I wanted to quit every day. I wanted to give up and go home at least once a week. But somehow, I hung in there.

Every person that I've ever known in my life who's really won big has paid a big price. But after they won, they all looked back over the price they paid, which seemed to be awesome when they were paying it, and they said, "You know what? I dreamed of how great it would be to be where I am today. I thought it would be wonderful and that kept me going through those difficult times. But now I've won, I find that winning is so much better than I ever dreamed. If I'd known how wonderful it is to win, I'd have paid 100 times the price."

Push-Up Principle

Paying a price builds confidence and staying power.

One of the special benefits of paying the price is that, when you give something your all, when you really work hard and sacrifice, it builds both your ability to do something well and your mental attitude.

Vince Lombardi once said, "Fatigue makes cowards of us all," and a former coach of mine believed in that. He made us all practice in these big, heavy-topped shoes instead of our soccer shoes. And, he made us run our "wind sprints" at the first of practice instead of at the end.

His theory was that you went out and got really tired — and then you began to practice. He believed that if you could do things right when you were tired, then you could win football games. We practiced hard, and we'd get so mad. We'd fuss and fight about how cruel our coach was. But, when we went out to the game, we died hard. That coach had us ready to play. We were a tough bunch of dudes, I'll tell you that, and we won a lot of football games. Champions are the hardest losers, because they sacrifice the most. They have more to lose than other people, so they won't give up. Once you've gone out there and paid the price and sacrificed, you build a toughness of attitude that just won't let you quit. And, you build the kind of confidence that comes from knowing you're prepared.

After we played in those heavy, high-topped shoes all week, we'd put on our football shoes and we'd feel like we could dance. We weren't tired at all, the way we'd been at practice, and we felt like nobody could beat us.

When you really work hard, and you're really prepared, you develop an expectation of winning. You know you're ready. You know you're going to succeed. And that's a wonderful feeling!

Chapter 16

Do It First

Management Mistake

Some managers see themselves as delegators instead of "do-ers."

Leadership Solution

Leaders never ask anything of their people that they wouldn't do themselves.

These three little words, "do it first," house one of the most important concepts of leadership. On every winning team, in sports or business, it's easy to recognize the team captain. He's the one who comes in early and stays late. He's the one who keeps on working and keeps on believing during the worst crises. He's the one who does everything first, before he asks his team members to do it.

In our company, I like to use the phrase, "Do it—then talk." Because, you know, everybody can talk a good game. Everybody can tell you how you ought to work and how you ought to live. But talk is cheap. What your people want to see from you is *action.*

As a leader, you should never ask your people to do something that you haven't done yourself. I'm not talking about specialized jobs, where you hire a person who has expertise that you don't have. I'm talking about asking for time, energy, effort, and commitment from your people that you don't have yourself. We all know of a case where the boss knocks off at 5 o'clock, leaving the employees behind to finish a project. If you want your people to perform, you have to turn in a performance yourself that's as good — or better — than the one you ask for. I believe in the kind of leader who goes out and does it, leads by example, and then talks about it.

It's the simple old idea of "setting an example." If you're trying a new sales approach that you think will produce big results, don't send your people out in the field to test it. *You* test it first, then show your people the great results you've received. The interest you get in the program will double, and you will have sold the idea to your people.

If you've had big success, they're going to be willing to try it, too.

So many leaders today like to see themselves as "idea men." They think their job as a leader is to have lots of good ideas for their people to go out and try. A word to the wise: nothing is cheaper than a good idea. Taking action to carry it out is the important part.

Push-Up Principle

People will follow whatever example they have — good or bad.

Whether you want to or not, you are setting an example for your people to follow. If you aren't setting a good example, you're probably setting a bad one!

The easiest way to set a good example is to work harder than anyone else on your team. Do that, and the battle to be a good leader is half won. Someone once said, "There are no office hours for leaders." How true! I'm not saying that you have to be obsessed with work, but it's a fact that real leadership just isn't a 9 to 5 job. It takes effort above and beyond the call of duty, every day, all the time.

A very successful manager in our company confided his story to me about his close brush with failure. He had a big, booming sales organization, filled with people he had trained. As a salesperson, he was the best. As a recruiter, he was just about unmatched. Yet, after several years of building a successful business it suddenly began to flounder. The more he pushed his people, it seemed, the more unresponsive they became.

Finally, he realized his problem. After years of leading his people by being the best salesperson and the best recruiter, he had put that aside and become an administrator. His business was big, and there was a lot of paperwork. He had begun to spend more and more time in his office, and less and less in the field with his people. It was an innocent mistake. He thought that was what he should be doing; he thought it was time for him to move on up.

But he was wrong. Holing up in your office and removing yourself from the playing field may look to you like stepping up to a higher position. To the other people living on the playing field every day, it looks like you've abandoned them. Luckily, our manager realized what was happening before it was too late. He divided the office paperwork between all his managers, giving them that portion that dealt with their business, making them responsible and teaching them administrative tasks they needed to know. This also freed him up to get back out where he belonged — with his people.

Avoid the "behind-the-desk" trap. Whether you're leading a sales force — or a room full of accountants — be where the action is, and take part in it. Do everything you want your people to do, *first*. Then talk.

Push-Up Principle
Ultimately, you must win.

As a leader, you've got to do it right, and you've got to do it first. But there's one more critical thing. Ultimately, you must win. You can understand the needs of your people, you can treat people good, you can stand for something, but ultimately, you must prove that you are a winner. If you treat your people right and work hard, you'll gain their respect up to a point. But the fact is, nobody wants to follow a loser. If you don't win eventually, their respect will begin to fade, and ultimately they'll begin to wonder why they should follow someone who's not successful.

Winning legitimizes all of your talk. You've been telling your people they can be successful; you've been explaining what an opportunity they have to succeed. At some point, they've got to see an example of that success.

As I go across the country, I counsel with a lot of husbands and wives who are involved in our business. So many times I find that the manager is down in the dumps and the spouse is upset. The husband has come to work with our sales organization, and the wife is at home with the children or maybe holding down a job, too. The husband is excited, because he's started out in a new area, he's excited about the possibilities for success. He just can't figure why his wife isn't excited, too.

Usually, the problem is that the spouse is terrified of living on a commission income. She's nervous about whether or not they'll have the money they need to support the family. When I hear this complaint from our sales people, I often give them this simple bit of advice: "If your spouse is unhappy, go double and triple your income. If she thinks you're crazy to be in the sales business, go make $10,000 in commissions this month, and I promise you the spouse's attitude will change."

I always get a few chuckles with this, but it's really so true. It's the same with your people. If your spouse, who wants to love and support you, has trouble believing your "success" is for real, imagine the doubts your people have. They are depending on you to lead them in the right direction.

Many companies promote a concept of, "Fake it till you make it" to their managers. That's so ridiculous! You can't drive a car that you can't afford and expect people to believe you're successful. Your people know you too well.

Push-Up Principle
People need to see "local success" to keep them motivated.

If you want to keep people motivated and excited, you must have local success. It's not good enough for your company to do well. Your people have to be able to see individual people doing well, people who work with them.

Your people can't relate to general success, or the success of people they don't know personally. They must see someone close to them succeed — someone they can feel, touch and smell —before they can see it happening to them. That someone should be you — their leader. Before your people will believe that victory will come to them if they keep working, they have to see that you have done just that, and won.

Push-Up Principle
Your people need to see your winning spirit.

If you are on the road to winning right now, but still can't quite show your people true success, the thing you can do is show them a winning spirit. You can make sure that they know you intend to win, and that you intend for them to win, too.

Tennis great Chris Evert Lloyd had something to say about the mental difference between winners and losers. "The top players just hate to lose," she said. "A champion hates to lose even more than she loves to win."

If you haven't really won yet yourself, work hard to get there. And in the meantime, let your people know that you think like a champion. Let them know that you won't accept losing; winning is your game plan, and you're on schedule to win.

Don't ever fall into the trap where you say, "Well, it's really not winning that's important, it's how you play the game." How you play the game is important, of course. But don't ever kid yourself that winning isn't important. Somebody once said, "If it doesn't matter whether you win or lose, why do they keep score?"

So get out there on the playing field with your people, do it first, do it best...and win. They'll be right behind you.

Chapter 17

Build With Quality

Management Mistake

Many managers are in such a hurry to build their business that they do things the quick way instead of the right way.

Leadership Solution

Never sacrifice quality; there's no substitute for building it right.

139

There are two ways to build your business or your career. You can build it in a hurry, using any method that works. Or, you can build it the right way, with quality. Building with quality takes longer, but it's worth it. Quality is important in all areas of your business, for one big reason — quality *lasts*. Often, hasty methods work for a little while, then fall through when you're least prepared.

Learn to think "quality" in every area. Ben Franklin said it best. "Being ignorant is not so much a shame as being unwilling to learn to do things the right way."

Push-Up Principle
Never let your desire for rapid growth take the place of your common sense.

I see it happen all the time in our business, especially with new leaders. They start out cautiously; they want to build a thriving business, but they're afraid of making a mistake. Often, they're extremely careful when it comes to hiring someone into their business.

Then, as time goes by, they get more comfortable, they're having good success, and they get a little lazy about devoting the time it takes to find really good people.

If a leader gets lazy about hiring, he will eventually find himself with nothing more than a bunch of warm bodies — not to mention a million problems. It's a shame so many people have to learn this lesson the hard way.

Now, I'm not talking about looking for "credentials" in people, like college degrees or fancy upbringing. We've talked about those things already. I am talking about taking the time to select people who will perform for you, people with extraordinary "want to" who have a burning desire to build their own careers. Those people aren't going to walk into your office just every day and tap you on the shoulder. You have to be aware and you have to take the time to look for them.

There will be times when people you thought were real "studs" will turn out to be losers. Some will lose interest and quit. But, the point is, you've got to keep looking for the right kind of people, people that you think can do the job. You can't hire a bunch of people with bad character or poor potential and expect them to work out. You may grow faster, but your progress is bound to be temporary. Reckless building will always come back to you in the form of bad business and financial loss.

Your people are your greatest resource. Don't treat the hiring process casually. It's one of the most important things you do.

Push-Up Principle
Work with those who deserve it, not just those who need it.

On the surface, this sounds like a harsh principle, but it's not. It *is* a tough principle.

Every person who comes to work for you in your organization needs your help. A big part of your job as a leader is to help people get started, train them the right way, and stick by them through both good and bad times. But, eventually, there comes a time when you have to back off and let people rely on themselves.

Over a period of time, you'll see who is really making the effort, really trying to make it in the business. And, you'll see pretty quickly who is making no effort at all to succeed. As a leader, you have to work constantly to help the people who are sincerely trying to succeed, the people who are trying to help themselves. You can't spend all your time working with people who will not meet you halfway by putting forth effort of their own. Every leader, sooner or later, must make that distinction.

That doesn't mean you just give up on the people who aren't making an effort. You must always encourage, always be positive, and always keep telling them you think they can make it if they're willing to try. But, at some point, you have to leave the burden of effort to them. You have to stand back and let them show you they're serious and sincere, and that they have the determination to succeed in your organization.

Too many times, I've seen people take the role of leader to the extreme. They get so involved in trying to help build successful people that they wind up spending all their time trying to motivate people who are doing nothing. Meanwhile, the people who do have the desire and are willing to work hard lose their momentum through sheer neglect and lack of direction.

Remember, you only have 24 hours in a day, and there is a limit to your time. Help all your new people equally and watch for the "do-ers" to stick their heads up. Then, focus the majority of your attention on helping those who are eager to improve and want your help.

I'm not saying that you should give up on people — never! Always be willing to help and always encourage everyone to work toward their full potential. Let your people know that you'll never "write them off." But always remind people that you cannot become successful for them — they must do it themselves, with your help. You can only help those who will help themselves.

Push-Up Principle
Give your efforts time to compound.

I've never seen this principle in print before, but I believe that it's a critical one for building your business. Everybody talks about effort and consistency and hard work, but nobody talks about the importance of *time* in building a business or career. I see so many people who work incredibly hard, then give up before they've really allowed enough time for the seeds of their work to bear some fruit.

It's just like the principle of compound interest. You put $100 a month in your savings account and that $100 draws interest, then the interest draws interest, and it keeps on compounding until you build up a sizable sum of money.

It's the same with your efforts and abilities. I've heard people say, "It doesn't matter how hard I work, I'm not ever going to become a success." What they don't realize in the early years of their business is that, even though they may not be making a lot of money, they're developing their talents and accumulating knowledge.

True, all that knowledge and development may not pay off today or tomorrow, but the more you do, the more you keep building your talents and your wisdom. Eventually the payoff will be more than you ever anticipated — both in terms of money and in terms of incredible business success.

Compounding is important in personal relationships, too. All the people you meet during your business career, all the personal contacts you develop along the way are an important part of your career. The person you meet today may be just the person your business needs five years down the road. Or, you may be just the person he needs 10 years down the road. The relationships you build throughout your business life can pay off richly in terms of personal satisfaction, as well as important career development.

When your business is going good, don't decrease your efforts. Keep moving ahead. In fact, intensify your efforts or you'll lose the advantage of the compounding effect. Just as you have to keep adding to your bank account to take advantage of the compound interest, you must keep building in your career to keep the compounding effect in force. If you slack off for six or eight months, you'll feel the difference two or three years later.

The only way you gain real knowledge is through effort and experience; there just isn't any other way. People have a tendency to discount the importance of sticking with one career area for a long period of time. They get impatient for success and jump around from one thing to the next, never allowing time for their efforts to compound.

Always remember that everything you're doing today will pay off for you in the future — with interest.

Push-Up Principle
Always be willing to start over.

Because it's tough to lead your own business or organization, you're bound to make mistakes. Everybody does, and some
mistakes hurt more than others. Sometimes, a mistake may
seriously damage your organization, and you may lose
everything that you've worked so hard to gain.

One characteristic that I've observed in winners is that they
are capable of starting over, if they have to.

In our business, I've seen people who folded at the first sign
of defeat. But I've also seen dozens of people suffer devastating
setbacks, then pick themselves up and begin again from square
one. It's been my experience that these people eventually make
big successes of their businesses and their lives. They have the
ability to turn the biggest mistakes into wisdom that helps them
build it better than ever the next time.

It's a fact of life that people learn very little when everything
is going well. Most great lessons, in business and in life, are
learned in the hard times. Being able to survive those times builds
the kind of inner strength and character that people who always
have it easy just never know.

Be willing to start over rather than compromise your
principles. If a business deal would move your business ahead,
but involves unethical practices, don't do it. If eliminating a
problem or terminating someone will cause you to lose money,
do it in spite of the money. Even if you'd like to just close your
eyes to the problem, you can't. As the leader, you've got to
handle it.

A note about terminations: I believe in being very slow to
terminate people unless they do something illegal or something
that jeopardizes the company or hurts its people. I will always try
to give a second, third and fourth chance.

Yet, I know from experience that sometimes it's una-
voidable. It's always a tragedy, but a leader must look for ways to
create something positive even in a negative situation.

A few years ago I was forced to terminate someone in a high leadership position. He had three managers who reported to him and I immediately promoted them. They were excited with their new position and increase in income, and they brought positive leadership to the group. All of a sudden, I had three happy, productive people and a positive situation to replace the bad situation.

Always be prepared to start over one more time if you must. The best reason to do it is that you have to. The only other alternative is to quit.

Quality in every aspect of your business is an important concept. In my opinion, the only way to build it big is to build it right. It takes a little bit longer to build your business or organization with quality — quality people, quality methods, quality principles — but it's worth it. You'll have fewer disappointments, a stronger business, a better feeling about yourself and your people, and bigger success. And isn't that what it's all about?

Chapter 18

Always Move Ahead

Management Mistake

Some managers get fired up for a few months, then slack off, depending on how their business is going.

Leadership Solution

A good leader keeps moving ahead constantly, regardless of whether conditions are good or bad.

The sales business is a business of momentum. I know that because that's my business. When I was a coach, momentum had a lot to do with success there, too.

Leaders recognize the importance of keeping up momentum in their business. It's one of those things that's hard to describe. It's hard to say exactly what momentum is, but you sure can tell whether it's there or not. Momentum is happening when everybody seems to be doing something. There's lots of activity; something's happening every day; there's a total involvement in the business that includes everyone.

When momentum is in your favor, you must "get all you can get." That's the time to increase your effort and activity. The law of nature says that, eventually, the momentum will go the other way. You see this happen all the time in athletic events.

For example, a coaching friend of mine was winning a basketball game by a huge margin, and he began to feel a little sorry and embarrassed for the opposing team. He began playing his second and third string players. The momentum suddenly swung in favor of the opposition. By the time he put his first string players back in they were "cold" and couldn't get their momentum back. My friend's team ended up losing the game!

The same thing happens in business. When your business is going good and momentum is in your favor, there's a tendency to relax and enjoy it when, in fact, that's the time to become even more intense in your purpose.

An important part of the leader's job is to always keep that momentum, to keep moving ahead constantly, steadily. If you ever allow activity to come to a standstill, it's three times as hard to get it going again.

Push-Up Principle
Always keep your activity up.

In our company, we have a phrase that we use to indicate activity in a sales organization. That slogan is "Keep them coming and going." In our business, it means bringing in new reps, training them to be managers, and spinning them out to form their own organizations. But it means more than just that one thing — it means keep your activity up, all the time.

In any thriving, growing organization, you'll find a lot of activity. I love to go into an office where people are running around like crazy; phones are ringing off the hook, people are talking to each other, some are running out the door, others are running in. It may seem like chaos, but you can tell that something is happening there. On the other hand, when I go into an office and everything looks real formal; people are all sitting kind of quietly at their desks, the phones aren't ringing, I start to wonder if anything at all is really being accomplished.

One of the most successful people in our industry says, "You must have 90 percent organized confusion to constantly grow." I agree.

Most of the time, you can tell what kind of leader is in charge by the type of office environment you see. If the leader is an active, aggressive person, chances are that the people in his office will be the same way.

As a leader, you set the tone. You are ultimately responsible for the activity of your organization. One of the most important things to develop as a leader is a sense of urgency. You've got to tell yourself that this is the time to do things in a big way — not tomorrow, not next week.

One of my own biggest faults is that I'm not very patient. I want things done yesterday. But I've tried to channel that impatience in a positive way. I've tried to develop it into a sense of urgency that helps our company do as much as possible today, right now. If you try to see how much you can accomplish in one day, at the end of a week, or a month, you will have made more progress than you ever thought possible. Don't let you and your people get into the old trap of "we'll do it tomorrow." Do it right now. Why wait? Your competition isn't waiting.

Push-Up Principle
Think big. Don't major in minor things.

How many times in your business life have you started out the day with a list of "to do's" that you planned to accomplish, only to find at the end of the day that you hadn't done a single one? All of us get sidetracked from our main purpose from time to time. But, if you're not careful, you can spend two-thirds of your time doing things that are secondary to your main purpose.

In the sales business, making sales is the number one task that needs to be done each day. But I see so many people spend a lot of unnecessary time on paperwork and all sorts of administrative type tasks instead of making sales. They work very hard, put in long hours, but at the end of the month they earn a pitiful income because they never actually got out there to make their sales.

Don't worry about administration. I never saw anyone fail because of administration, but I've seen hundreds of people fail because of lack of activity. Time and time again, I've advised salespeople to spend the money to hire a secretary to handle the administrative details. They can easily pay that salary from the money they earn making all the sales they've been missing by not being out in the field.

Once I was at one of our company conventions and we had a presentation by one of our leading administrators. He spent an hour discussing how to read pay statements from the home office, something the sales people had specifically asked for. The longer I listened, the more frustrated I became.

When my turn to speak came, I told the sales force that I felt that was the most wasted hour of the entire convention. I reminded them that we have a multi-million dollar computer system and dozens of administrative people who are experts at figuring pay statements. Ninety-nine percent of the time, the pay statements are going to be correct. Plus, I pointed out, if a sales person is really getting after it, if he or she is out there making as many sales as they possibly can, they're going to have so much money that it won't even matter if one sale doesn't get credited correctly. I've been in the business fifteen years, and I still can't read a pay statement. I never took the time, because it's not that important to know how it's calculated. What is important to me and my family is making the maximum amount of sales possible in that week.

I'm not saying you shouldn't be interested and careful about your income. But the people who spend hours each week, checking and rechecking their pay statements to make sure they haven't lost a dime, are losing hundreds of dollars in sales that they could be making during those few hours. That's majoring in minor things.

Analyze carefully what activities are going to build success in your career, and concentrate on those things. Don't let the minor things drag you down. And remember, your people are watching you. They will concentrate on what you seem to think is important.

Push-Up Principle

Your people don't have time for a lot of meetings. Neither do you.

Meetings are the single greatest time wasters in the business day. Friday morning meetings, twice-a-month meetings, daily meetings — American business people seem to think that they're supposed to have meetings, whether they need them or not. It's even gotten to be a status symbol. The manager who spends his whole day in meetings is viewed as "pretty big stuff."

I know that sometimes meetings are necessary. But having a meeting just for the sake of having a meeting is dumb. Pretty soon, they lose all their impact. People don't see it as something important, it's more like "Ho hum, another boring meeting."

What's wrong with calling a meeting only when you do have something important to discuss with all your people? I'm a firm believer in emergency meetings. Whenever something important comes up at our offices, I call an emergency meeting immediately. With emergency meetings, your people will quickly realize that something important is going to be discussed, and they'll come prepared to get serious.

Emergency meetings can also be motivational. If there's a problem you need to discuss with your people, this type of meeting will establish the sense of urgency we were just talking about. People get fired up, they want to do something, and they leave the meeting prepared to take action.

Push-Up Principle

To keep your organization moving, you've got to keep track of your people.

The activity of your organization depends on the activity of your people. As a leader, you have to monitor that activity. I've tried different methods, but my experience has taught me that there's only one way to do it effectively. You've got to spend time with your people, eyeball to eyeball.

As the president of our company, I travel about three days each week to different offices around the country, or to management gatherings that we hold in a centralized area. All the traveling gets pretty old sometimes, but I really have no choice. How can I possibly expect to know what's going on in the company if I don't get out there and see what's going on? Nobody else can give you the kind of information you get just going to an office or some type of gathering and talking to the people, one to one. Nobody can tell you about the activity in a given area like the people who live there and work the area every day.

You'll be amazed what you can learn face to face with all levels of people in your organization. You'll find out about problems they're having, and maybe be able to give some advice; you'll find out what that group of people is doing well, and get some ideas you can pass on to other groups.

If you're having problems with activity, think about how much eyeball to eyeball contact you have with your people. It could be the problem.

Push-Up Principle

You can't do it all; teamwork is essential to an active business.

This is a good place to talk about one of the oldest concepts in business-teamwork. The key to any organization's success is working together for a common goal, as well as a lot of individual goals.

No one person's strengths are enough to make an organization run well and succeed. You build a healthy organization, not only on your strengths, but on the strengths of others. Nothing can take the place of shared goals and commitments. It gives your people a sense of companionship that means a lot in any business, particularly the sales business.

Encourage friendly competition among your people. Get people interested in competing for the top production or the most recruits or the most sales made in a week. Little and big competitions are fun. They encourage people to work independently, yet for something that benefits the entire organization. At our company, we have a lot of contests that encourage people to compete with each other for several top slots. We allow for several hundred people to win, so a lot of people get rewarded. The competition is fierce to see who will be number one, number two, and so on. Offices and whole regions vie against other regions to see whose team will perform best overall. Besides the friendly competition, goals get met, and it keeps activity high.

Develop a team atmosphere, and focus on the contributions of every member of the team. You can't do it all yourself, and you won't have to if you keep everyone involved.

One more thing about teamwork. Nothing adds new life to a group of people like new blood. The excitement and enthusiasm of a new person, experiencing your organization for the first time, will remind all the "old-timers" of the way they felt when they first joined the company. And, you may find that all the old-timers don't want to be outdone by the new person and will want to make a good showing for them, so they'll work even harder. New people bring excitement, and they stir things up. Bring in new folks all the time, and watch the movement start in your group.

They'll believe what you've been telling them all along about how great they are and once they're convinced of that, they're really on their way!

Keep moving forward. When you keep your activity up, you'll have the momentum it takes to advance even when conditions are less than ideal. As long as you never stop, defeat and failure can never catch up with you!

Chapter 19

Remember The Giving Principle

Management Mistake

Some managers forget their responsibilities to their people when they begin to succeed.

Leadership Solution

Leaders never forget the power of "giving" in their personal and business lives.

I believe that the practical principles in this book will help you to keep moving ahead in your career. As you experience success, however, there's one area that I believe is essential to your being able to keep growing. Failure to remember and follow this principle can hurt your future development more than failure to follow good business principles.

You've probably heard the theory that people in management eventually rise to their own level of incompetence. I don't believe that's true. It would truly be a sad situation if everyone reached a point in life where they could no longer succeed, no longer grow or no longer accomplish more. Yet we all know of cases where people work for years and achieve a level of success, then seem to reach a point of frustration, disappointment, and unhappiness. It seems that their development has stopped, and their success has begun to fade. I've observed this a lot in business, and I believe I've finally figured out why this occurs.

Push-Up Principle
Don't catch the disease of "self-ness."

Famous psychiatrist Alfred Adler said, "It is the individual who is not interested in his fellow man who has the greatest difficulties in life and provides the greatest injury to others. It is from such individuals that all human failure springs."

I believe that people get to a low point in their careers or their lives because they've begun to let "self-ness" rule their thinking. They get to a point where they can only think of the world in terms of how it relates to them. "I" and "my" dominates their thinking, and becomes more important than "you," "the working colleague" or "the team."

It's not that the person lacks the ability to succeed in business and in life; more often he lacks the confidence and belief in himself. As a result, he sees the success of other people as a threat to his own, and loses the desire to share his own success and his ability to enjoy the success of others. He stops living for other people and begins living only for himself.

I believe that the self-centered person will eventually reach a point in his life where it is impossible for him to grow and be happy. His energy becomes directed inward, and he loses touch with the nourishing powers of other people. Eventually, this kind of self-ness will sap him of his energy and pleasure.

Push-Up Principle
Follow the "Giving Principle of Life."

LUKE 6:30 says, "Give and it shall be given to you." I believe that simple statement is the key to being able to keep moving forward and growing in both your business career and your life.

By giving to others, I don't mean giving money or material things. In business, I think giving those kinds of things only delay people's problems. I do believe in giving your positive attitude, your loyalty, your commitment, your faith in people, your winning example, and your will to win. By giving your talents and your energies to your people, you help them reach a position of independence — and I think that's the greatest thing you can do for anyone.

If it's true that life will defeat a person who lives only for himself and his personal satisfaction, then it's also true that that same person will get strength, energy, love, happiness, and success by giving to others. The person draws strength from those he seeks to help and from the act of giving itself.

Another aspect of the "giving principle" is that the more you give, the more you receive. The more people you help, the more people will come your way. This is more than just a moral principle. It works in the practical business world, too. One of the main principles in the free enterprise system is that the rewards of success go to those who provide a better product or offer a better service to people. The more helpful their product or service is, the more benefits they will receive in terms of success.

Push-Up Principle
Give without expecting a return.

As a leader, you are constantly trying to motivate people to give their time and effort to your business. Do that by giving to them first. If you help other people get what they want for themselves, you will receive those same blessings. Often, when we try to help somebody, we want them to be grateful — in fact, we expect it. But the Christian ideal of "It's better to give than to receive" also applies in working with people. If you give of your time and efforts generously, and from the heart, you've done everything you can for that person. If you recognize that your joy and fulfillment is in the giving, you won't be frustrated or disillusioned if that person doesn't respond.

Again, it's the same thing you do with your family. You give your children everything you have to give, freely from your heart, but there comes a time when they have to take what you have given them and make it on their own.

Do everything you can. Never stop giving, but when people disappoint you or turn against you, realize that you gave it your best shot and go on to help the other people who need help. And, if the person who disappointed you wants another chance, give again.

I promise that if you give your efforts with that attitude in mind, nothing will keep you down for very long. And as for rewards, you'll get plenty from the people who experience success.

"Pushing up people" must become a sincere way of life —coming from the heart —otherwise it won't work. It must be genuine.

You need not fail in your personal or business life, especially in your leadership of people, if you are truly interested in your fellow man. Express that interest by trying every day to push up people.

Never Give Up

Management Mistake

Many people get discouraged and quit before they have a chance to win.

Leadership Solution

A leader sees adversity as a challenge and keeps on going.

If you set your priorities and goals, build with quality, keep moving ahead and follow the leadership principles I've outlined in *Pushing Up People,* you're on your way to a wonderful work experience. Nothing can stop you now! Nothing, that is, except *you.* You always have the power to stop yourself from succeeding by the simple act of sitting down and quitting. That's why I've saved this principle for last — because, after all is said and done, nothing is quite as important as not giving up. The ultimate "secret to success" is that you can never be defeated if you never stop trying.

The saddest thing I see in business is when someone with great potential and great talent gives up before they've given themselves a chance to win.

In a way, you can't blame people. It's tough to win in business today. It's always a struggle, and there are a million disappointments and frustrations along the way.

But, so many times, things look worst just before they start to turn around. People give up at that worst moment, only to find that if they'd waited a few more days or a few more weeks, they would begin to see their efforts pay off.

A winner never entertains the idea of quitting. A winner makes a decision to win, he builds himself and his business toward winning, and he never — *ever* — gives up.

Push-Up Principle
Winners are made, not born.

No one is born a winner. People make themselves into winners by their own efforts.

Winners come in all shapes and sizes. Talent, IQ, experience or education are not requirements for winning. Winning is an internal thing, something you decide to do and direct your efforts toward. So is losing. God doesn't make losers. Losing is something you learn to do all by yourself. But, the best part is that you can decide to become a winner at any time, wherever you are in your career, even if you've been a loser all your life.

Most people do almost enough to be a winner. They stop short of winning because their attitude, or determination, or desire, falters. But once you make a total commitment to becoming a winner, nothing can make you lose.

Winning individually, and helping others win, involves a lot of different elements. We've talked about many of them in this book. But most of all, winning involves a personal decision. If you don't make that personal decision to start winning, no matter what it takes, you can do everything right and still fail. If you don't help your people make that decision, all the other things you teach them and do for them will be useless.

I learned this lesson from an experience in my coaching career many years ago. After college, I was an assistant coach for two years at Thomasville High School, one of the great football schools in Georgia. I wanted a head coaching job so bad I couldn't stand it. One day the principal called me in and told me that he thought our school's coach was leaving, and he wanted me to be the next head coach. I couldn't believe it! I was so honored.

I went immediately to the head coach and asked him about it. He told me he had had a couple of offers, but he thought he was going to stay in Thomasville.

In the meantime, I had been offered a head coaching job at a school in Baxley, Georgia. It was a small school with a very weak football program. With spring practice coming up, they were pressing me for a decision, so I left Thomasville and took that job.

A few weeks later, I heard that the head coach at Thomasville had left to take another job. I was devastated.

But things were destined to get even worse.

It was tradition for the previous year's team to play the new team at the end of spring practice. The old team had won only one game the previous year. They had no coach, and they didn't even practice to prepare for the game. I was so excited, because I knew that our team was going to beat them about 100 to nothing. All the townspeople were coming to see the new coach at work.

What they actually saw was the graduating seniors beat our pants off. I sat on the sidelines and wanted to die. I couldn't believe I had gotten myself into this situation! I saw my whole life being ruined. I could have had a school with the finest football tradition in Georgia, the kind of team that wins eight or nine games just by showing up. But here I was, caught at a tiny school with a team that couldn't win.

We went off for a weekend, and I think I cried for two days straight. I was in a mess, and my football program was in a mess. Then I realized that my team might not be the number one team in Georgia, but they were depending on me. I could bemoan the fact that all I had was a 150-pound tackle, but it wouldn't get me anywhere. They believed that I was a winning coach, but I hadn't returned that faith. I had to change my attitude about their ability and potential.

I went back to school the next Monday, and I called my little team together. I told the kids, "You know, when I came here, I told you that nobody expected us to win. The only people we had on our side were the school and the townspeople. As great as I thought our opportunity was, I think it's 10 times greater now. Now, nobody expects us to win." I promised the team that we were going to surprise everybody, we were going to do something great.

After that, I started doing anything I could think of to build a little pride. I bought weights, and started a weight training program. We ripped out the lockers and put in new ones. We painted the dressing rooms. Most important, I began to treat them like winners.

That summer, when the other teams took off, we met every day and lifted weights and practiced passing and kicking the football.

We won our first game and our second, and continued to improve.

In the fifth game of the season, we faced the number one team in the state. Even though our team had improved, they were way out of their league against this team. I felt that it would be a major victory for us if we could hold the team to a 28-point loss.

But that wasn't what happened.

Only six months after our humiliation on the spring practice field, that team beat the number one team in Georgia, and gave me one of the greatest thrills of my life. The team that nobody believed in at the start of the season, including me, went on to become one of the most talked-about teams in the state.

Those kids taught me a lot about faith and determination and the "will to win." And I learned a lot about how the attitude of the leader can affect the members of a team. They didn't start out that practice season as winners. If anything, they had a history of losing. I had to change my attitude of seeing them as losers and help them to see themselves differently. I pushed and encouraged them, and they built themselves into winners. I became a coach and in that short six-month period, a group of losers died, and a new batch of winners was born.

You know, we all get to a low point in our lives; we all hit the bottom of the barrel. That first practice game in Baxley was the lowest point in my professional life. But when you get to that point, you've got to decide whether you're going to be frustrated and bitter, or fight and compete.

My team in Baxley taught me that you can come back from those low points; you can rise above what everybody says and thinks and decide to become a winner, in spite of the biggest obstacles.

Push-Up Principle
Good people outlast bad times.

One of the special characteristics of winners is that they never think that they haven't got a chance to win. Even in the toughest times, they just never see themselves losing.

In the early days of our company, we had a sales leader in a little Southern town who was starting to have good success. Unfortunately, our competition had enough clout in the local political system to cause us a lot of aggravation. Finally, things got really bad. Local officials were persuaded to enforce a "cease and desist" order which put us out of business in that state.

The order was reversed after only 10 days, but it wasn't over for the man who had worked so hard to get his business going. During the 10 days, there were major stories in local newspapers. About 80 percent of his people quit, rather than face the controversy. It was a crushing experience.

But this guy didn't throw up his hands. He simply started all over again, with more determination and conviction than ever. It wasn't easy, but he recovered totally from what most people would have seen as a "no win" situation.

Today, our company writes more business in that state than our top 10 competitors combined, and the man who stuck it out is now a multi-millionaire.

There are many people in our company who have been an inspiration to me because of their refusal to give up. People like these:

— The man who, after a year of struggling in sales, took a paper route to pay the bills until he could make it in sales.

He got up at 5:00 a.m. to deliver his papers before coming to his sales job each day, and he never gave up his dreams of owning his own business and becoming financially independent. Today, he's a gifted salesman and a millionaire.

— The woman who was left with four children to support, no income or savings. She struggled for four or five years before everything started coming together, but she stuck it out. Today, she, too, is a millionaire, and has fulfilled her family obligations better than she ever dreamed.

— The man who joined our company following a divorce and a business failure that left him $250,000 in debt. He refused to declare bankruptcy, because he didn't want to skip out on his commitments. Several years later, all his debts are paid, and he's a millionaire, too.

We could all take a lesson from these people. All refused to give up. They knew that they could become winners if they just kept moving ahead, and believed in themselves. They set the kind of examples for their people that inspired respect and loyalty. They were winners in every sense of the word.

Winners know that the tough times never last. Sooner or later, if you try hard enough and long enough, it's going to get better. If you give up, you've lost any chance you had to win. Quitters are good losers. You quit once, and it becomes easier to quit the second time. Pretty soon, quitting — not winning — has become a habit. Why not let winning become a habit instead?

Almost everyone knows the story of Abraham Lincoln. Here was a man whom anyone would have said had no future at all. His family was poor, and he had little encouragement to succeed. The pattern of his life is a monument to perseverance:

1831 — Failed in business.
1832 — Defeated for legislature.
1833 — Second failure in business.
1836 — Suffered nervous breakdown.
1840 — Defeated for elector.
1843 — Defeated for congress.
1848 — Defeated for congress.
1855 — Defeated for senate.
1858 — Defeated for vice president.
1858 — Defeated for senate.
1860 — ELECTED PRESIDENT.

Lincoln had more failure than most of us have. But he was never really defeated, because he never stopped trying to succeed.

Once you experience how it feels to hold on during a tough time, and beat a bad situation, you'll know what pride and confidence are all about. It's so nice to look back on the rough times that you survived and realize that you didn't fold up. It's so sad to look back on the tough times and say, maybe for the rest of your life, "I could have been somebody special, done something special, but...." Before you can become a winner, you've got to become a survivor. The times will get better. You have to keep getting better, too. When your situation looks bad, remember the words of our great president, Franklin Roosevelt. "When you get to the end of your rope, tie a knot and hang on."

Push-Up Principle

Don't make an emotional decision about your career.

One of our company's leaders made a very wise statement in a recent interview. When asked how he kept going during the tough times, he mentioned a simple rule he had applied successfully during his career. "Never make a decision about your career based on what happened today."

We can laugh, because we've all had "those kinds of days," but I don't know when I've heard a sounder principle. At those times, the temptation to just toss it all in can be overwhelming. During my career, I've wanted to give up a million times. Some days I'd say to myself, "It just isn't worth it. Life's too short to put up with this kind of stuff."

When you're really frustrated and ready to give up, don't act on it that day or that week. Keep plugging away for a little bit longer after you think you've reached the quitting point. Very likely, something will happen to make you see things differently.

When you see one of your people getting in that kind of state, you can help by encouraging him to talk about his problems and frustrations. That doesn't mean you have all the answers. It may not even be the time for advice. Many times, someone who's upset just wants someone to listen to his problems and be concerned about what he's going through.

Push-Up Principle

A situation is only impossible if you think it is.

"Impossible" isn't a condition, it's a state of mind. You only have to look at the way in which people have overcome incredible odds to realize that almost anything is possible if you set your heart on it.

I love the story of runner Glen Cunningham because it exemplifies the kind of refusal to admit defeat that makes champions different from other people.

Cunningham was in a terrible fire when he was only five. The doctors told his parents that the burns on his legs were so severe that he would never walk again. He would have to spend the rest of his life in a wheelchair.

But the doctors didn't know about Cunningham's determination. He vowed he would get out of bed and walk. And he did. He practiced constantly, using an old plow to hold himself up. Step by step he dragged his legs along until they would move on their own. Once he was able to walk, he wanted to run.

And he did run, faster than anybody ever had, as a matter of fact. Cunningham went on to become a great mile runner, setting a world's record of 4.00.68 in 1934, and was named as the outstanding athlete of the century at a celebration in New York.

Most people would have given up in the kind of situation Cunningham faced. But he wouldn't accept being beaten. Again, it's a matter of attitude. If you think a situation is hopeless, it probably is. If you think it can all be worked out, it probably can. There's just no way I can over-emphasize attitude. If you've got a winning attitude and you've decided that you're in the game until the last whistle blows, you just won't consider quitting.

My best advice when you feel that the odds against your success are impossible is to work a little bit harder. Sometimes, for things to improve, you must improve. It may take more effort or more experience or more "guts." But if you keep on trying you can catch up with the odds and turn them around.

Push-Up Principle
Have the courage to at least try.

An American writer once said, "All glory comes from daring to begin." The worst way to fail is by never getting started. You may lose, you may fall flat on your face, but before you can accomplish anything great, you've got to have the courage to at least try.

Seven years ago, when we founded our company, I took a hard look at myself and I just didn't like Art Williams.

Everybody gets to that point at some time. I wanted to be able to look at myself and like who I saw. I wanted to be able to say, "You've made a contribution. You've lived a good life."

But seven years ago, I looked at my whole life and I was just sort of sick. I was average, or a little bit better. But I didn't feel like I had done what I wanted to do in my life. Then I realized two things that really shook me up.

First, I realized that life doesn't always give you a second chance. You think life is going on forever, and you'll have unlimited chances to start over. But you only get one chance at life, and that's it.

The second thing I realized is that, if you look at how long you're here in relation to time, you're here for just a flicker. Your time on this earth is so short it's unbelievable. I started looking at my life and I said, "My life is racing away, and what have I done?"

When I started out, all I wanted to be was a good athlete. I worked harder than most kids, and I was a little bit better than average. But now I realize that I took so many things for granted. I didn't think about my future. I thought those Friday nights on the football field would go on forever.

As an adult, I wanted to coach football, and when I got my first coaching job, I was as happy as anybody in the world. But as I looked back at my coaching career, it was the same old thing. I had a good career, but it wasn't what I wanted it to be.

Even though I loved coaching, it wouldn't support my family, so I gave it up and went into business. My first seven years, I was better than most, but not great. The same old thing again. Meanwhile, my life was ticking away.

I sat down and asked myself why I had so many regrets as I looked back over my life. And I think I found out why. I believe I wanted to be somebody so bad — I wanted to be happy and successful, I wanted Angela and the kids to be proud of me, I wanted people around me to feel like I was the kind of guy they'd like to have on their team — that I was afraid of failing.

In my heart I was scared that maybe I wasn't going to be able to be a winner, that maybe I couldn't succeed. I was so afraid of that happening and not being able to face myself. To have to live with knowing you're a loser would be a terrible thing. What if I had to admit that I had to be average and ordinary? I couldn't face that because I wanted to be somebody so bad.

I realized that my fear made me hold something back. Rather than give it my best, I said, "Well, if this thing works out, great, but if it doesn't then I just haven't found my 'thing' yet." That was a ready-made excuse.

But time was running out. I got so miserable with myself that I finally decided that, even if I didn't win, I was going to go out there and try. I did go out and try, and I became somebody that Art Williams is proud of. That's important to me. Whether anybody else is proud of me or not, I'm proud of myself. But I almost didn't make it simply because I was afraid to really try.

People ask the question, "If you had your life to live over, would you change anything?" Man, I'd change a whole bunch of things. I'd work so much harder. I'd be so much better. And I'd enjoy everything more.

I'm lucky, because I realized, before it was too late, that the thing that I was missing was the courage to try. You've got to have it if you're ever going to win in a big way. If you've been holding back, let go soon and really give it all you've got. You'll never be fully happy or fully satisfied until you do.

Push-Up Principle
Leadership is everything.

This book is about being a leader. If you've decided to take on that leadership role, you now have awesome responsibilities, and awesome opportunities, as well. No one can make other people's decisions for them, but a great leader can literally change people's lives by encouraging them to build their lives into something they're proud of, and by offering the support, love and dedication that people need in order to "keep on keeping on" when the going gets tough.

Every great person can look back on his or her life and credit a lot of what they've accomplished to someone who influenced their life in a positive way, someone who encouraged their dreams and helped them set a standard of excellence. Everyone remembers one person who believed in them, even when they didn't believe in themselves.

You can be that person for your people. And, if you are going to be a leader, you have a duty to be that person. If I have gotten any point across in this book, I hope it's that leadership is not a role to be taken lightly. It's not a hat you put on in the morning and take off in the afternoon. It's a full-time, seven day a week, permanent job. It's the most responsible job in the world. It's also the most rewarding.

I hope that the principles in this book will help you become a great leader. I know that they have proved more valuable than gold to me in my own efforts to lead.

In a position of responsibility, you *will* influence people, either for good or for bad. I encourage you to become someone who is an example of "never say quit," someone who's the kind of leader that others will be proud of.

Index

Index

Chapter 20 — Never Give Up

Acknowledgements

Acknowledgements

Writing this book was a very emotional experience for me because, in many ways, it's the story of my life. As I look back today, I see now that it was impossible for me to fail because I had so many people who continued to push me up. Those were the very special people that I remembered as I wrote *Pushing Up People.*

My Mom and Dad — they were very positive examples in my life, and always made me feel special and important.

My high school coaches, Coach Tommy Taylor and Coach West Thomas — they were the most important figures in my life, outside of my family.

My hometown, Cairo, Georgia, a small south Georgia town of 10,000 — Cairo provided me with the perfect environment. The town's commitment to youth was unbelievable.

My former assistant coaches and football players — we won by building a team on the principles in this book.

The A.L. Williams people — the most committed, most dedicated, and most courageous people in American business today.

My children, Art and April — even when we were living on $100 a month while their mother and I were finishing college, they made me feel like I was the best Dad in the whole world.

My wife, Angela — the single most special person I've ever known and the greatest partner a person could ever hope to spend his life with.

My friend, Dona Janeway, one of A.L. Williams' most valuable executives, and the person most responsible for helping me make *Pushing Up People* a reality. Dona and I spent hundreds of hours together talking about the difference in winning and losing. Without Dona's insight and fabulous ability, there would be no *Pushing Up People!*

Arthur L. Williams, Jr.
Founder
A.L. Williams

Arthur L. "Art" Williams, Jr. grew up in the south Georgia town of Cairo. He learned a lot about winning from his father, who coached football when Williams was young. Art, Sr., along with Williams' two high school coaches, encouraged his dream of one day building his own coaching career.

He earned a Bachelor of Science degree from Mississippi State and a Master of Science from Auburn University.

After graduation from college, Williams began a highly successful coaching career, which included two "Georgia Coach of the Year" awards. As a coach, he began to learn how to tap the tremendous potential found in all people. He came to realize the importance of individual success to team effort, a concept that would later serve him well in the business world.

In spite of his coaching success, Williams dreamed of financial independence and of having the opportunity to do something special with his life. He was introduced to basic financial planning by a relative and became intrigued with the "buy term and invest the difference" concept. In 1967, Williams began selling term insurance and securities part-time and became increasingly committed to the concept.

In 1970, he made a big decision — he left coaching, moved his family to Atlanta, and went full-time with an insurance and securities firm. Over the next eight years, Williams rose from agent all the way to regional vice president. At each level, his staff led the company in production. His positive attitude and his philosophy of "treating people good" earned Williams respect as a leader.

In 1977, Williams fulfilled another dream — he founded A.L. Williams with 85 friends and associates. It was a company designed with the needs of the consumer in mind and built on the "people management" philosophies developed throughout his athletic and business career.

Today, A.L. Williams is the largest marketing organization in the world, producing more than $92 billion in business and breaking nearly every record for a new company in the largest industry in the world. The original 85 people, working out of eight offices in three states have grown to more than 195,000 people, with offices in 49 states, D.C., Canada, Guam, Puerto Rico, and the U.S. Virgin Islands. By "pushing up people," A.L. Williams has produced over 100 millionaries and thousands of financial success stories.

Williams formulated the concept of "people power" throughout a lifetime of leading others, both on the athletic playing fields of Georgia and the playing fields of the American business scene. Through *Pushing Up People* Williams hopes to promote the incredible power of positive, motivated people.